ANGEL
of Islington

ANGEL
of Islington

Psychotic creativity against a
backdrop of cerebral insanity

IOAKIM ELEFTHEROS

THE CHOIR PRESS

First published in the United Kingdom in 2015 by
The Choir Press

ISBN 978-1-910864-02-9

Preface

*T*racking and tracing one's insanity via reflective, recollected thought processing is challenging. Voids are eventually filled as you trawl through the jigsaw puzzle of your life.

Nevertheless, the halcyon decay of innocence and profound insights into the mind's furthest reaches can best be described as enigmatic, despite initially appearing problematic.

Kaleidoscope colours and magical backdrops should be what it is all about and not how much we earn nor how much we acquire.

When you resolve your internal conflict, the clarity of vision will guide you through life.

As humans we face many challenges and we persevere through them to achieve closure. Do not get caught up in the result. Enjoy the journey. Ultimately you will find peace and harmony whilst travelling down your path – accidental or mapped.

The Author

Sent Mail Item

Hi Dr — , just finished reading An Unquiet Mind *– brilliant!*
Inspired me for something – will discuss @ our next catch up.

One

'Hi, Uncle. An Englishman asked me to seek somebody I knew in Greece so that I can obtain a Greek passport.'

'Don't worry. I've got you!'

A rush ripped right through my body as I hung up the telephone. Total exhilaration! I had never felt so alive. The tone in my uncle's voice was authoritative, soothing, reassuring and made sense of my whole life up to now. At the time I believed that I was destined for a remarkable journey; however, I had no idea where it would lead me or where I would end up. I just knew that my time had come.

So I headed off to the UK, with a wife, flourishing career and the only way up!

Life has a funny way of having its way with you despite best-laid plans.

Arriving in London was an interesting experience as my EU status allowed me easy passage through customs. My wife, however, had to endure a process of interrogation – albeit friendly – regarding not obtaining a work permit, as per the then-current EU work visa conditions. I explained clearly and patiently to the customs officer that I was seconded to the UK via my employer and that they had not advised me that my wife – of non-EU status – needed to obtain a work visa. Customs detained us for a little while before releasing us into the crisp morning air. The customs officer was polite and favoured my logical reasoning and allowed us both passage into London, based on obtaining additional documentation from various embassies within the next month or so. His fixed, yet friendly, gaze made it clear to me that he knew who I was and that he would not interfere with my journey. He understood how important I was in the grand scheme of things. I also realised, though, that I would be a marked man in London and that my every word and step would be monitored granularly.

So, my new employer put us up in Pimlico, London, pending my wife and me securing our own rented accommodation. The stay was for two weeks or so, and I enjoyed the suburb. It was a very conservative place, with many restaurants, beautiful gardens and a library nearby. It was a relaxing period and I would grow fond of Pimlico.

During our stay at Pimlico I did begin to notice that people were looking at me with an odd gaze. It was a flat, rather unimpressed, look. It felt a bit strange that the majority of the people I encountered were like that. The best way to explain it is that it was like a facial stand-off. As eyes met there would be no smile or look away, just a strange non-connecting experience. It would continue to be the norm for a very long time.

I remember dining out in a restaurant in Pimlico once and feeling absolutely miserable. Although the ambience was nice and the food was passable, the waiter gave me a strange look whilst taking my order. I tried to maintain eye contact with him but his face seemed to distort as I was looking at him. I could not connect with him and in my mind put it down to getting used to the new surroundings and not being familiar with the general mood of London. This distorted image of people's facial expressions recurred many times. It was not quite a hallucination. It was just hard to explain at the time and I just could not figure it out. This frustrated me.

Looking back, I experienced a similar sensation upon our departure from the closest airport to our marital home, en route to the United Kingdom. The duration of my tenure, which was two years, ensured that a considerable amount of family and friends had gathered to see us safely on board our flight. As we were heading off to the customs

—ᴇᴏ—

clearance section, I looked back at the gathered crowd and they seemed to shrink right before my eyes. Their faces seemed different to their normal appearance and their configuration was slightly distorted. It was hard to resolve in my mind and I just put it down to my profile naturally rising. It was as if I had swallowed their mind space and they just had a blank, soulless, lifeless look in their eyes. I had sucked up all their knowledge and thoughts in that brief moment, like something straight out of a science fiction novel. It was weird and yet it made me feel stronger and invigorated!

A similar occurrence transpired riding the London Underground, whilst residing in Pimlico. There was a vagrant lady who was waiting for the same train as my wife and me. I made her out from the crowded platform as her presence seemed literally highlighted amongst the backdrop of commuters. At the time I believed that I possessed the power to read her mind. I was trying to explain this ability to my wife when the vagrant fixed her gaze upon me. She was, of course, trying to place ideas into my mind whilst I was trying to read her mind. Her profile overpowered my mind and I could not continue to hold a gaze with her. I felt a stabbing pain across my right eye. I looked away as her face also distorted. I tried to explain the occurrence to my wife in logical terms; however, I am sure that she thought there was something odd about my commentary. I outlined how the vagrant lady was trying to offload her pain onto me as I had stared at her uninvitingly. My wife dismissed my ramblings on the spot and we hopped on a train and continued our tube ride.

That night in Pimlico there was an electricity blackout and our whole apartment complex was without power for the night. I stood outside the apartment in the freezing night air, where I spotted an elderly lady a couple of doors down. She was almost crying and muttering something about being alone. Should I approach her and comfort her? I could feel her obvious sadness and pain but resisted the temptation to intervene. Not only could I feel her distress but it upset me beyond belief. What kind of a cold and unwelcoming place was I living in? Big-city loneliness? Maybe. But this was a different altruism. I could see deep into her soul and could reconcile her thoughts and feelings. At the time it spooked me a little. I would, as time went by, learn to master the craft of mind reading.

Take that overwhelming sensation back in time and I believe that it occurred similarly when I received my pre-high-school scholarship – as it was known at my school. During the last term of my last year of primary school, about ten students, including myself, were selected to take part in a series of final-year examinations to determine the school's best academic student. I did not study much, but with an accelerated passion for academia and knowledge I felt prepared. I would end up winning the scholarship comfortably. There was an ad hoc school assembly called and we all wondered what it was for. Someone must have been in big trouble! As we gathered I noticed my parents on the makeshift stage. I was in trouble? I thought to myself, *What did I do for my parents to attend?* They had been pre-advised of my scholastic success and were asked to be present. My name was read out by the principal and I headed towards the stage. As I elevated my small frame on the temporary landing, I gazed in wonder at the crowd before me and they seemed to shrink in stature. It was like I was a superpower. The elated feeling I had was not normal. It was paranormal.

My first official day of work in our London office was also rather odd. I was dressed in a navy suit with a striking tie and white shirt. I cut a very sharp figure meeting my line manager at reception. He was a charming Englishman with a great middle-class English accent. He was resplendent and suited up with fashionable braces and our first eye contact was one of mutual respect. I had gained favourable attention in the company, as a gifted executive, and my reputation preceded me. Toward the end of our ten-minute catch-up I was fixated with his gaze, though. The mutual admiration had diminished into almost resentment at the way he was looking at me. I felt him overpower me with a superior profile which made it difficult for me to maintain a normal conversation. I dismissed him and these thoughts in my mind with a mental, and somewhat violent, disassociation within the confines of my private thoughts' sanctuary.

I recall conversations with the middle-class English manager during our regular catch-up for coffee, tea or lunch. He would outline his grandiose aspirations of eventually becoming the managing director of the UK organisation over the next five years. He was structured, logical and analytical and openly shared his insights with me. I thought it was slightly bizarre as we had only just met and for all intents and purposes he was planning a succession overhaul. Was I supposed to assist him in reaching his goals? He was candid with his career aspirations and I must have come across as a powerful potential ally. He was building a team and I was being groomed as his right-hand man.

I also opened up to him. I asked him why he chose me for the position when the Oxbridge crew were almost literally breaking the company's door down. He just smiled and stated that he liked me and my personality. I came across as easy-going and relaxed and it suited the collective profile he was trying to populate with new talent.

Our unit had a meeting during my first day, in one of the many available conference rooms. As I was being introduced to my new team members I found that I could not maintain the status quo of the mood and was feeling increasingly superior in mental strength and presence to the whole team. When asked by my manager, 'Any words for the team?' I answered in a rather twisted tone, 'I'm new here, so be nice to me.' My manager cast a quizzical look directly at me and there was momentary silence. No one responded, as I must have taken them by surprise. I had just blurted out the first thing that came to my mind. Upon psychotic reflective analysis, I believed that I was subconsciously laying down the law regarding my treatment during my tenure. Don't mess with me!

My first day also happened to coincide with a team lunch at a nearby Thai restaurant. During lunch I loosened up with some drinks and got to know my colleagues better. Losing track of time, I forgot that my wife had returned and would be waiting for me at the office reception at a mutually agreed time. I was going to be late. I was indeed late in returning from lunch. My wife was not impressed.

It was not the first time I had been late. Prior to my UK secondment and during our stay in our marital home, I had left the house to buy some cigarettes. I returned fifty-one minutes later and my wife was not sure why I had been late in returning. I explained to her that I had been driving around our neighbourhood to clear my mind.

The fact of the matter was that when I had left the driveway, in my fully maintained company vehicle, I had been overpowered by a sense of adrenaline coloured with pure vitality, zest and an amazing tingling sensation filtering through my entire body. This manic state made me feel very physically empowered and tranported me to another place. I drove erratically and had to explain to a police officer, who had just pulled me over, why I was all over the road. He had been following me for the majority of the trip. I advised him that it was due to using my hands-free mobile phone and he let me drive off with a warning. Countless roads were travelled on much later, in multiple countries. It was the only way to clear my mind – driving and listening to music.

Two

Where do I start?

My first recollection of my mood disorder is of the television viewing of a FIFA World Cup final match at a friend's house. There were about four of my friends gathered to watch the game. I remember it clearly and vaguely. I had always followed football vigorously and my favourite team was Liverpool. During this screening I felt as though the players involved in the match were not quite in synch with my view of the game. It felt a little abnormal and I found it a little difficult to watch and follow. It was as if the camera angle had been altered and the view I was receiving had become disjointed. So much so that I remember commenting to a colleague during a pub session, whilst I was living in the UK, that I was upset that the camera angle had changed during a historic point in time. I knew why the angle had been altered but did not share the secret with him. I actually believed that a Belgian international striker had over-celebrated a goal and for this reason the camera angle was adjusted. Why? Because the Belgian striker's profile had risen against the accepted norm of transmittable and documented live coverage and 'the governing authorities' were given no choice but to adjust the camera angle to 'contain' the new level of the profile.

Now let us log on to the World Health Organization (WHO) and see what they have to say:

Overview: Depression is a common illness worldwide, with an estimated 350 million people affected. Depression is different from usual mood fluctuations and short-lived emotional responses to challenges in everyday life. Especially when long-lasting and with moderate or severe intensity, depression may become a serious health condition. It can cause the affected person to suffer greatly and function poorly at work, at school and in the family. At its worst, depression can lead to suicide. Suicide results in an estimated 1 million deaths every year ...

Bipolar mood disorder: this type of depression typically consists of both manic and depressive episodes separated by periods of normal mood. Manic episodes involve elevated or irritable mood, over-activity, pressure of speech, inflated self-esteem and a decreased need for sleep.[1]

In my case, long bouts of depression would be followed by long periods of mania – an energised existence with incredible feelings of elation. I believed that these highs and lows were just my normal personality profile. I would continue functioning in a depressed state for months at a time and then suddenly I would wake up happy and energised. As my illness progressed, the highs and lows became more polarised with more frequent catastrophic impacts. They would progressively become my total insanity.

During the early onset of my disease I would say that I was occupying a depressed state, rather than struck down with depression. Alternatively, during the manic phase I would be bubbly and engaging. As the depressed state was not severe enough to disable normal teenage tasks and rituals, I did not analyse it too much. I knew that I would 'snap out of it' in due course as this was the normal cycle of events. The manic state was just around the corner and I knew that the promise of this energised state would see me through the depressed state.

*

---

[1] World Health Organization, 'Depression' (http://www.who.int/mediacentre/factsheets/fs369/en/), October 2012 (accessed May 2015)

I was a fairly accomplished guitar player, so music was important to me. In my younger teenage years and during the 'down' phases I would create music with lyrics which were dark, bleak and helpless. One tune was titled 'Here Comes the Rain'. The music and lyrics met the same fiery death as all of my 'non-core' endeavours. I would literally burn many creative works so that controlling forces could never trace them back to me. At the height of my illness I was mentally wrestling with voices that were ordering me to destroy all material addiction to be totally free. This included my complete creative works. Bonfire of the Insanity! Here is a snippet from my memory banks:

> *... When I see a child cry out*
> *I know that all alone I cannot stop his pain ...*
> *So stop all your fighting,*
> *All your conditioning,*
> *Because you know that I'm not listening,*
> *I don't need to borrow,*
> *I don't need your sorrow,*
> *I know that I'll be fine,*
> *Because after all the sun, here comes the rain ...*

And of course there were the happier manic times where my songs were full of summer breezes and spoke of hope and love. I wrote this one and performed it at our wedding whilst on the cusp of a psychotic high. I cannot remember the title, and, yes, the manuscript turned into sprinkled ashes, like everything else. A fragment from the remaining library in my mind:

> *... Do you remember a long time ago*
> *When we used to play out in the snow?*
> *We used to laugh, sing and cry a lot,*
> *Always together no matter what ...*

So take me by the hand
And I'll make you understand . . .
That all I want to do is be in love with you . . .
I'll take you away to the Promised Land . . .
As all I want to do is be in love with you . . .

There were also the bizarre moments in between mania and depression, where I would glide metaphorically into purgatory and varying degrees of anarchy. This mood was hard to explain but best summed up by a song I wrote titled 'All the Same':

. . . You catch the morning train,
You go to work and it's all the same.
You're looking for a love affair
But who it is you really don't care.
You knew someone like you once
But now it's over, no more fun,
No more love and no more hate,
Only indifference awaiting fate . . .

My outstanding grades, with hardly any study and under strict examination conditions, gained me entry into an academically leading university. I lasted less than six months. This was mainly because I was experiencing a depressed state. It was hard to concentrate and I did not care for university much. It was not the utopia I had envisaged. In fact, I clearly recall my last lecture. A beautiful young lady sitting next to me asked to borrow a pen. I said, 'Here, have mine.' It was my only pen. That was the last lecture I attended, and I walked straight into student administration and withdrew from the course. I spent the next month or so playing in nearby gaming arcades when I should have been in class, as I did not have the heart to tell my parents I had dropped out of university.

During a mildly depressive period and shortly after school, I was working within an organisation (the same organisation that seconded me to the UK) and I wrote a poem titled 'Death by Politics'. I was twenty-one years old. Many, many years later, after returning to my parents' home from the UK and Europe, I burnt the only copies of this and other poetry I had written. I was clinically insane when I destroyed the poetry. To this day it is my single biggest regret. The passages were haunting and beautiful. Try as I might I can only remember fleeting, fragmented passages.

From 'Death by Politics':

... Oh! Mother, Mother, I have not forsaken you.
It is Death's Door I approach, something new.
You always evoked curiosity of the worst kind.
It is now my own future I try to find ...
Everything I do, I do for your saving,
Perhaps a little frightened of my own decision-making ...
You always marvel at a freshly bloomed rose
But I only grimace about the menacing thorn ...
In time, I am sure you will come to understand
That it is to a long-lost friend I lend out my hand.
I have nothing left behind at all,
Only a grain of sand so meek and small.
Oh! But I cannot stand the increasing pain
Embracing a soft cushion that my blood will someday stain ...
Can a man have it all
And still remain a creature brave and tall? ...

And yet there is one passage which frightens me until this day, from 'Death by Politics':

... I cannot despise but I can learn to dislike an image of me
That deals out these cruel blows and still insists belief in Thee ...

The above line frightened me because during the height of my illness I heard it read to me by a female voice in a vivid colourful dream. It wasn't an ordinary dream. It was a schizophrenic dream! The voice was clear, digitally enhanced and did not resemble the tone of spoken words during normal dreaming.

During the milder manic-depressive phases, life was, as I thought, very normal. Friends, girlfriends, casual affairs, sport, solid working career, trips overseas and music – I played guitar regularly and tinkered on the piano. I was, however, constantly searching for something. I did not know what it was at the time. The meaning of life? Maybe! All I could see was a metaphoric distant light at the end of a tunnel. In fact, when interviewed for the UK gig I was asked about future career plans. I answered the question routinely with regard to progression up the organisational hierarchy, but also mentioned that I was drawn to this distant light. I also mentioned in the interview that in my role as a young upcoming executive, prospective customer relationships would be easily established and nurtured. As the interview concluded, I told my interviewers that I would see them soon. How arrogant was I? No decision had been made at that stage and I had left them with no choice but to give me the position, which I had virtually bulldozed myself into.

It was not the first time I had applied for the London job. I had contacted the UK office previously, but they had not had anything available at the time and the UK Human Resources director had politely directed me to apply via the local HR channels. When I ended my stint in the UK, it was this same HR director who felt the full force of my resignation. I wished at the time to plaster the image of my superior mind all over his inferior profile. As my last corporate breath escaped from my mouth, I released my natural speaking voice in a calm, philosophical and matter-of-fact tone indicating where I believed they had failed as an organisation. There was relief from all concerned but they must have been overwhelmed by my honesty and cutting words.

Three

In my virtual state I believed that I had a heightened sense of awareness and self and I would show it off at any given opportunity. I even recall stating aloud in the London office one day, 'I am not afraid of anything.' This self-belief manifested in an essay which I addressed to some philosophical organisation recounting the 'Higher State of E'. I was shopping at Sainsbury's one day and processing random thought, when all of a sudden my thought shut down and there was nothing there. Literally nothing. It lasted all of sixty seconds and was quite surreal and a little scary. I came to the conclusion that I had elevated my mind to an altered state of consciousness and that I could now shut down normal thought analytics. Try as I might, I could never recalibrate my mind-mapping to a point where I could repeat the occurrence. The title of the essay was a subtle reference to the search for true empowerment. A theme which would plague me for a very long time. I was seeking the true meaning of enlightenment and I found it, accidentally, in a supermarket chain. But why Sainsbury's? I would end up doing all of my grocery shopping exclusively at Sainsbury's from that point on.

Around the time of composing 'Death by Politics' I had taken a trip to the United States with two friends. During this trip we attended the House of Horrors wax museum in Los Angeles. We purchased tickets and as soon as I entered the place I was literally shaking in fear. I felt a presence that I could not explain. In my mildly insane mind I acknowledged this as pure evil. I could not wait to get out of there. Whilst the wax figures were not scary to an adult, there was something about the geographic location which registered as evil to me. In my mind I processed this location as demonic. My friend asked me why we had to leave so soon. I made up some excuse about having a headache and we headed back to the Sunset Strip. I was comfortable in the Strip even during the early hours of the morning. Even back then I was processing locational aesthetics as either good or evil.

As the disease accelerated in its manifestation, this would not be the last time I would feel a sense of threat from a location or point in time, nor, for that matter, of elation. This was exemplified when my wife and I were honeymooning in the USA. We were staying with relatives in Long Island, New York, and we would frequent Manhattan Island daily. One trip included a day out hopping across many of New York City's famous sites. We soaked in Greenwich Village, Little Italy, Chinatown, Wall Street, the Empire State Building, Trump Plaza, Radio City Music Hall and many other premier locations. As we headed towards Times Square I felt a rush come over me. I arrived in the heart of the city and what I believed at the time was the centre of the world. I was jumping out of my skin. It was, and I was, so full of life and vibrancy. In my mind I punched in the co-ordinates and decided then and there that this was the place where all magic happened. The place where life would happen and which was the absolute known superpower on Earth. It was like a supernova and had celestial qualities. I did not wish to vacate the location. I was enthralled and naturally wired.

After soaking up and literally draining the location's core aesthetics, my wife and I had to return to Long Island and decided to take the Long Island bound train from Manhattan Island. We had spent all of our money and only had credit cards and one travel token. We realised this just as we arrived at the station. The token or ticket would unlock the gate and allow for entry onto the train. It was single file only and of course one passenger per ticket. I told my wife that we were going to bend the system a little and we concluded that she would go first and I would follow immediately after, before the gate had closed. I looked at the ticket attendant, and just when we planned to carry out our misdemeanour he deliberately looked away and we passed relatively easily through the automated gate with a single ticket. Many years later I would dream about the ticket attendant's act of generosity and would feel his presence any time I required support on public transport. Cool Americana!

I would also bend London's famous double-decker red bus system in a slightly more blatant manner. Returning from a day's shopping in central London, my wife and I decided to take an alternative route and catch a bus home. She had a ticket but I did not and under no circumstances did I believe that I needed one. So I summoned all of my inner strength, thought of my American public transport friend and walked straight onto the bus. The driver momentarily paused but I stared him down and he continued the bus journey. He was a very large lad and either he could not be bothered arguing with me or I had overpowered him. Again a rush ripped up my spine and I felt vindicated in my decision. My wife remained silent. She had witnessed the whole scenario unfolding and was not sure what to make of it. I would repeat the public transport bending on an Athenian route, departing from the city centre towards my uncle's residence. Why? Because I could and it gave me an overpowering thrill!

When a bipolar sufferer tries to analyse their condition logically, during the height of their illness, it is important to note that although the thought process is not normal, the sufferer believes that this insane state is normal for their individual mind and personality. In my mind, despite being aware of a rising profile, I was internally justifying my thought to myself. How could it not be normal? I could not diagnose my thinking as bizarre because I was rationalising my actions and thoughts. In hindsight, an untreated condition like mine could easily have led to destruction or death itself.

You need to understand that I had no reason to believe that I was not normal. From my perspective, I just happened to be accelerating in development and power. I also believed that all of the circumstantial and coincidental evidence around me was substantiating my theory.

Whilst working with my company, and prior to arriving in the UK, I did notice rapid changes in my thoughts and views. I would hold grudges for long periods over very simple misunderstandings. I remember that a very close friend of mine was late in returning some compact discs he had borrowed from me and we barely spoke for years. I would recall the fallout many years later and extricate myself telepathically from the situation by offering an explanation for my actions. He – my friend – was accidentally controlling my mind by having articles (my CDs) which belonged to me. I needed them to be returned to me so that I could continue functioning normally and not be held back by any person.

I also recall an office email exchange with a senior manager from another team over a work-related matter. He was considerably older than me, intelligent and a recognised power broker in our organisation. Whilst the emailed communication was ordinary enough, every time I hit 'send' or 'receive' it felt as though our profiles were merging or morphing, if you like, into one identity. I sensed that I was overpowering him without being able to control my thought pattern. He was considerably more hierarchically senior than me, but it felt like I had sucked up all of his corporate knowledge during that afternoon's email exchange. It was empowering and a little frightening. It occurred during the week before I flew out to London. I had been temporarily promoted prior to heading overseas. I am still unsure why they bumped me up a rung as it must have been difficult to work with me, or, for that matter, for me. I was clinically insane at the time, just undiagnosed.

Months before heading off to the UK, I also insisted that my colleagues engage me by my full first name and not a shortened version of it. I was quite obsessive about the instruction to the point of demanding it. This was because in my mind it was important to be addressed by my name as I was a special person. It got to the stage where I was getting into arguments with my colleagues over non-compliance. This carried over to London and I insisted defiantly that I be addressed correctly – to the point of heated exchanges. Not every employee concurred with my view, and it created friction and a further distance between myself and the general daily contact I was having. Plummeting further and further into the self-created abyss, fewer and fewer traits of normality were remaining. I was over the edge and destined for a spectacular, calamitous fall! My parting quote to the team as I left for the UK secondment was, 'There can be only one!'

Four

After our initial stay in Pimlico, my wife and I settled on a rental place near Chalk Farm Tube. The property was introduced to us by a breathtakingly beautiful female real estate agent.

My wife had called this particular agency during the week and had arranged to view the property over the weekend. As we were setting off from Pimlico, I felt a presence, mentally and physically, come over me to wear my estate Audemars Piguet Swiss gold watch. It was an engagement gift from my wife. It was a beautiful piece. This was possibly and probably the first time I had encountered a physical schizophrenic episode – out-of-body experience – which involved direction to complete a task. During milder bipolar manic periods I did experience extreme energy levels which resulted in extreme sexual desire and extreme sexual energy. This was different. I was being forcefully instructed to do something by some unknown power. The force literally carried me to the kitchen bench where the watch was resting. I put it over my wrist and in my foggy, dreamy state caught the tube with my wife to the real estate agency near Hyde Park.

The designated female real estate agent was serving another potential customer, so we waited. When she had concluded her discussion she came up to where we were sitting and introduced herself. She had an accent.

'Swiss, French?' I said.

She said, 'Yes.' She glanced down at my Swiss watch and slightly knelt before us – because we were sitting down – revealing an open top. Her bra was visible and I checked her out deliberately. She did not adjust her pose but continued the conversation. She was our age and we felt very comfortable around her, and she was bubbly and engaging. Our eyes met and I fell in love with her immediately.

We arranged an appointment to view a Chalk Farm studio apartment. My new love met my wife and me at the address and showed us around. Like much of London inner-city living the apartment was tiny, cramped and expensive, but we took it as it was in a cool area and, after all, the agent had been so nice to us. We formed a friendship from then on. Our new home had nearby restaurants and all the necessary amenities. I enjoyed life at Chalk Farm.

During our stay at our new rental home, we arranged for an assortment of cutlery and CDs to be shipped from our marital home to the UK. It arrived. I finally had my CD collection. I needed music to function. For some reason I kept playing the same song, with headphones on, over and over again. I was fixated on one particular song for no apparent reason. I must have played it hundreds of times.

The reality was that I was spiralling out of control mentally and I could not process normal thoughts. The song fixation was one of many non-conforming behavioural traits which had plagued me historically and were now being entwined in my future, complicated mode of operation. Every aspect of my life was entrenched in a different dimensional perspective. Initially it felt like surrealism without the mysticism. It felt like I inhabited one giant vortex which was undefined and not understood by myself, nor anyone else for that matter. After coming to terms with my psychotic realisation, I insanely adapted to the ever-changing structure of my mind. I managed to control my newfound power and in my mind calculated all the necessary adjustments to survive and thrive.

In the beginning I would complain to my wife that everything seemed different. It felt like it was reversed or upside-down. I found it difficult to connect with anyone or concentrate for long periods of time. Getting increasingly introverted and paranoid, I kept on feeling that it was me against the world. I was actually experiencing depression at that point in time. It was getting very difficult to manage and control my thoughts and it was impossible to try and fathom what was happening to me.

It was Christmas time in Chalk Farm, and a married couple were visiting London and were going to stay with us for a week or so. The woman was my wife's distant cousin and the couple were recently married.

We went out to central London for some dinner during New Year's Eve. I recall the night clearly as I was in a very paranoid state of mind. Despite having fun at an inner-city restaurant I was feeling uncomfortable. The reality was I was feigning interest in the night and the company. They were getting annoying and I could not wait for them to leave.

As we walked the streets of London I could not share the city's end-of-year festive mood and was feeling quite miserable. The yuletide greetings of the other night-goers whom we passed by were returned by me with a humbug frown. It may have been a special night but I certainly was not feeling it.

The four of us headed back to our flat in Chalk Farm and decided to play cards. The couple had a video recording device and were making sure they'd later be able to enjoy some memories of the trip by having the device on. We started a friendly poker game which was spirited and good-natured until I became obsessed with the fact that they were filming us during an unauthorised gambling session. I should state that we were playing with coins (small denominations). At the time I firmly believed that they were going to utilise the footage to show me gambling for money after

I became famous. This would then keep me from progressing up the corporate ladder because I had indulged in such illegal activities. The notion upset me considerably.

When they left the UK I discovered a solution to my dilemma. After much discussion and considerable distortion of the reasons, I eventually persuaded my wife to take an international flight with me for some holidaying. I brought my company-supplied laptop along with us on the trip. I sent the couple an email from an international destination stating that despite their having footage of me illegally gambling they should not use it against me. My country of choice this time was Portugal. I advised the visiting couple to stay cool! They did not respond. I advised my wife of the gambling dilemma and she told me not to worry about it. I did worry about it and it took me quite some time to get over it. If I was to catapult up the business tree I needed to be *clean*!

The daily work routine in London was difficult for me as I was constantly arguing with most of my colleagues. I could not connect with anyone, nor could I find peace of mind. I found it virtually impossible to concentrate. The charming middle-class manager was no longer assigned to me and I had a different manager to report to. He was a more working-class Englishman who was losing patience with my ever-increasing stupid antics. We were at each other's throats constantly. The arguments would carry over into universal themes and I would make massive issues out of trivial matters. In fact, we would always argue regarding the way client meetings progressed in terms of conversation threads. I felt he was dispositioning and belittling me in front of the client. I would not stand for it.

The heated exchanges were not confined to private meeting rooms as our gross debates became public office folklore. Many would side with me and many against me.

We had divided the office into two armies and I would not back down. I always felt that he was invading my personal space and not appreciating the notion of goodwill and respect. My assaults on him would take on grandiose themes and I would telepathically communicate my victimisation regularly. I was taking a stand on mind sovereignty and social injustice. In reality, he may have been difficult to work with but my rapidly deteriorating condition exacerbated the situation.

The UK division of our organisation had just landed a global contract and it was my job to manage it and grow the account. In fact as I recall I may have even been the one who eventually signed off on the deal. With great insanity comes great arrogance and confidence. Whilst my rhythmic logic had long since departed, my knack for business effectiveness must have remained or it may even have been enhanced.

Expedition of this global contract required frequent tube rides to our customer's location from our London office. The client had a soft spot for me and was the key decision maker. I was positive that in time he would have received a knighthood as he graced many company boards. He had warmth in his heart and would genuinely thank me after every meeting. I was a lot younger than he but we got on very well. It made me think that perhaps not all English people were stiff and bureaucratic. Perhaps some were warm and embracing, much like my champion of the boardrooms.

Even in my diseased state, I always maintained client respect and a great degree of business acumen. It just about got me through to the point where I could stay employed. My psychosis, however, had other ideas, and it was quite apparent that it would infiltrate any sane defences I had retained, and eventually tip me over the edge. It did, of course!

Five

During our stint in London, my wife and I would take weekend trips, as one does, to UK destinations and, of course, other European cities. One of those trips was a weekend drive and stay at Polperro. We had hired a car to get there. On the drive there I stopped for fuel and walked into the service station to pay the sum. As I entered the automatic doors, I sensed nothing in the shop. There was no mood and no smell and no feel to the place. The sole attendant had her head hung forward and I could not see her face, just a mass of long stringy dry hair. When she looked up, I was scared of her look. She had a death stare and in my confused state I thought she was life empowered without religion, organisation or family. This, in my mind, was what real empowerment looked like. A silent deadly look. I literally went pale. She had been placed at that service station to stop me in my journey and show what would ultimately become of me should I continue with my train of thought. Who would have placed her there? The powers who control the boundaries in life, of course. The same authorities who had changed the angle of the camera for the football television transmission. I had stumbled on a conspiracy. It would not stop me, though.

Another trip, another city. We headed to Athens, Greece, to pick up some visa-related documents at the British consulate. We stayed with my uncle and his family. The same uncle who had so exhilarated me over the phone prior to my arrival in the UK. I entered the lounge room and again there was no ambience, feeling, mood or smell. But this was true empowerment unlike the 'Deathly Polperro Empowerment'.

I chatted with my uncle in the lounge room and he

sensed that my non-Greek-speaking wife was uncomfortable. I translated to her to relax and be at peace. This was family. She would later return the same comment to me when we were holidaying in Milan, Italy, when I was uncomfortable in one particular restaurant. The location just freaked me out and we had to eat somewhere else that night despite just having ordered a meal.

During that first night in Athens I had a nightmare of the Polperro service station attendant, in which the vision of her face came to me across the window of our room. It was more than a dream as I could not decide whether I was awake or not. The next morning I saw a small stuffed bulldog wearing glasses on the coffee table.

We departed for the British consulate with prepaid tickets supplied by my auntie. We eventually made our way to the consular offices. I was a little bit disappointed that I had to ask for directions, as my auntie had provided clear instructions. The reason for the disappointment was because I believed that as a superpower I had risen above the requirement for maps and landmarks to locate places and could just sense where I was going.

The Greek security team searched us – standard procedure – and then allowed us to enter the lift to the British consulate. It felt as if they had been expecting us. Upon our entering the consulate floor there was a British national serving customers from behind a counter, wearing glasses. Another British national customer stated in a loud voice, 'All Greeks are thieves.' I did not flinch and my wife and I proceeded to the counter with our requirements.

The lady with the glasses turned to my wife, after examining some documents we had supplied, and stated in a quite forthright tone, 'Your husband is Greek.' She then placed her hand next to her forehead and left the counter. I had placed my first thought – accidentally – into somebody's mind and the result was a headache which she could not bear. I returned to my uncle's house and found the bulldog with the glasses dangling from an outstretched desk lamp by the tag wrapped around its neck.

That night I chatted with my uncle and his family regarding what I had been up to. It had been a while since I had last visited Greece. I tried to explain what I was experiencing at the time. I dared not trace out the exact detail of my thought processes. I advised my uncle in a cryptic retelling that my profile was rising and that I had amassed a small army of allegiance, scattered across the globe. He said that his friends were also scattered, but confined to the Greek state.

The message I wished to convey about my superiority was that it had happened naturally over time. Hierarchical employment success would have made sense out of my reasoning; however, I spoke in broad terms, somewhat thinking that he understood that I was achieving greatness globally. In my mind I was rising and I would soon rule the world and bear the financial return, position and power accredited to a demigod. I did not verbalise this to my uncle and his family – nor my wife – as I knew I had to keep it secret from 'controlling powers', because they may have ended my pursuit.

I told my uncle that I was trying to logically analyse my existence. He corrected me by stating that I was trying to complete my existence and fulfilment. He was right. Life is not two-dimensional. It is full of vigour and experience. What shapes you is what you become and cannot be achieved by a retrospective calculation of events.

My wife and I headed off for dinner to the upmarket Athenian suburb of Kolonaki. I had been to Greece previously and this was one of my favourite places in Athens. We decided to catch a cab as it was not too far from where we were staying. During the cab ride I had a fixed gaze and it must have freaked out the taxi driver. He reached a point very close to our destination and the taxi literally stalled. He stated he could not go any further. I felt my mind investigate the mechanical damage and resolve the issue without leaving the back seat of the cab. I could visualise the pistons, spark plugs and starter motor from my position in the cab. I was not afraid of my strength and felt supernaturally empowered. I advised the taxi driver that it was OK now and to restart the motor. It kicked in immediately. The cab driver went pale and slumped in his seat, causing the beads on his trembling seat to make an adjusting noise. He mumbled something about black magic and said he would not and could not go any further. We disembarked from the vehicle and continued to the nearby restaurant. My wife did not speak the Greek language and I dared not translate the details of the verbal exchange. Oddly enough it made me feel considerably stronger and I felt my global profile accelerating!

We continued our Greek adventure down the Peloponnese, ending up in Nafplio and Gythion. All the time I felt strong and gaining in superiority. These parts of Greece are beautiful and I was very much at peace here. It was a great experience and it was as if the locals were welcoming my visit with open arms. My wife and I were arm in arm and I was being guided by controlling forces with respect to turning left or right as we strolled down the cobblestoned streets of southern Greece. We would stay in hotels and dine out. All the time I could feel a presence guiding my meal selection, confirmed by the waiters' and hotel staff's acknowledgement of my great power proven by my dining choice. I had arrived!

Back at Chalk Farm, when we returned, life was fun – until I missed the remote control for our television. What had happened was that our Swiss-French friend had taken it when we had moved from Pimlico to Chalk Farm. It distressed me that someone else was holding on to a belonging of mine. She, of course, had innocent possession of it, but it was literally driving me insane. I believed that by having possession of a belonging of mine this person was gaining advantage over my mind.

During a work function at a nearby convention centre I popped into her workplace unannounced and asked politely for the remote control, after affectionately hugging and exchanging kisses on the cheek. She returned the remote control and I was relieved to no end. I was safe! A colleague from my London office was with me at the time and commented how beautiful she was. I told him that I knew that. I had to have her. I was totally wired at that point in time. I could not stop thinking and dreaming about her. Vivid, colourful dreams where we would be embracing and kissing passionately. I longed to be with her for eternity.

I would repeat a similar cleansing ritual, in reverse, endlessly at my parents' home. After eventually arriving from the UK, I returned many of my friends' acquired belongings by placing them on their front doors or in their letterboxes and driving away. I even returned cherished items I possessed to their rightful owners in the form of international mail. My Van Halen guitar picks, acquired at a concert I attended in San Diego, California, were returned to the USA headquarters of *Guitar Player* magazine. I did not wish to have power over anyone after what I had experienced with the remote control. With each registered mail item I felt another layer released from my heavy burden. I wished to be absolutely free and would go through every nook and cranny until I had filtered out any 'controversial' items.

My wife and I were invited to our Swiss-French friend's place for dinner one night in Notting Hill. We were going to meet her partner. He was Swiss and worked in the finance industry. We had a pleasant meal that night, with our new friends. She had prepared chicken fettuccine and as I recall a crème brûlée dessert – of course. During the whole night I was totally besotted with her and this must have frustrated my wife, because I literally wanted to have her then and there. I am sure we all picked up on the heavy chemistry. She was dressed casually but ever so breathtakingly attractive. I hung on her every word. Her dark hair, fair skin and alluring smile were all I needed. I was in heaven!

Every time I would see her in London for either coffee or dinner with my spouse, my heart would race uncontrollably. She would break up with her Swiss boyfriend shortly after the dinner. This excited and pleased me, but I knew nothing could eventuate whilst I was married.

Love and lust did not stop the demented thought process, though, as it continued unabated. One night, I mentioned to my wife that I had a moral problem with the résumé I had submitted for my UK assignment. My résumé contained reference to the completion of a junior extra-curricular sport, which was different to the one I had actually completed. The mistake had occurred because I had cut and pasted from someone else's résumé and in a hurry to submit the résumé had overlooked the mention. She said not to worry about it and that no one really cared. She was right, but for me it gravitated from a moral problem to pure obsession.

We had scheduled a trip to the south coast of Portugal for a weekend. I was so obsessed with the possibility of being caught lying on my résumé that I took a soft copy of my curriculum vitae with me to Portugal. It was a nice place and we were having a great time, up to a point. Prior to travelling to the Portuguese airport to return to London, we walked endlessly looking for an Internet café in Portugal so that I could resubmit my résumé from an unbiased international location. At the time I believed, because my personal brand was becoming global, I had to resubmit my curriculum vitae from a location outside the UK, to cleanse my apparent lying and secure the job position. The lie was the junior sporting reference in the résumé. I was obsessed with the idea that I could clear my name with an international transaction. I eventually hit 'send' on the email after much deliberation over context and phrasing. We flew into Heathrow that night.

Upon returning to the London office, I asked HR if they had received my amended, resubmitted résumé. They said no. I knew that they had.

A few days later the server crashed and non-critical business information was lost and unrecoverable. This included my résumé. I was vindicated. I had put so much pressure on the organisation that the information technology infrastructure had buckled under the grief which my heavy burden had caused. Now they would realise my true power. I could, inadvertently, push out thought that would corrupt software and operating systems. There were no limits to my power. I was also gaining in strength.

The next day the *Financial Times* had an article outlining that Portugal had just prospered financially within the European Union economy. I knew that they were waiting for me to visit Portugal to cement their economic position in Europe. I purchased a pair of shoes hand-made in Portugal to walk across those London streets. I would thereafter look out for Portuguese-crafted shoes.

Working effectively whilst you are psychotic is also, oddly enough, very difficult.

A female colleague and I were riding the tube to a client's office. I thought I could clearly hear what she was thinking via some sort of magnified mental portal. It sounded like, *Your Air Force will come and take you away from our offices. You are too powerful!* The words were scratchy and not normal. I did not flinch. She too was beautiful and we would argue regularly. I did desire her but resisted due to my marital status at the time. There was friction and tension between us. Her calming presence did assist me, however, during one hypomanic moment I was having on the London Underground.

On this occasion I was totally wired and could not find release or peace from an aggravated rising of my emotions. I felt anger. There was a group of three or four of us including this colleague and my working-class manager. I was arguing with the manager over something trivial and felt completely out of control. As I could not vocalise my insanity, I looked for some sort of inspiration to defuse the situation. I looked at my colleague and she lowered her eyes. She was wearing a necklace with a pendant. It was scribed with the word *LOVE*. This was as close as I was going to get to a change of mood. The British were too smart to release me from my frustration. In my mind they wanted me to crack and subside to the *system*. I looked at the pendant and broke into a smile and changed the subject. I was now taking instruction from accidentally-placed inanimate images and objects. This instruction needed to be random and needed to coincide with the situation as a magical release for me to accept it as real. Manufactured releases and deliberate placements of images and people were of no value. It was all about the meandering magic of colliding themes and events.

In hindsight, my work colleagues were tolerant of me. They would not have known, as I did not know, that I was psychotic. I was hired as an organisational leader to assist with a dysfunctional unit. I felt underwhelmed by the fact that I could not lead, but could merely argue constantly with the team. The arguments would also take on a global nature. I would insist that I could run riot because I was a superior being and that I did not need to maintain rank and file. Of course, it was always me against the world, or, more specifically, me against the British.

The vampire syndrome also made it difficult to maintain any mind processing continuity, logical or otherwise. At the time I tried to explain the phenomenon to my wife. This explanation was another illogical summation of thought, carefully yet insanely crafted into a logical theory. I felt as though British and French nationals could suck up your soul and thoughts instantly. During this event you could literally feel your face peel off. Whilst my wife encountered the sensation of her skin peeling, it was more like a hot flush rather than the nonsensical event I had methodically tried to explain. I believed that it was my wife's and my task to stop the vampires from leaving us lifeless. They could place thoughts into our minds and strip back all of our conditioned profiles. I had to kill the vampires and restore unadulterated, free-spirited human thought.

Whilst in France or England I would view vampires via mirrors and reflecting windows. I truly believed that I could nullify their power by engaging their reflections through various mirroring devices. I had to look at these devices whilst the blood suckers were unaware, to have the greatest impact. It was a tedious, obsessive and compulsive process. Much like flicking the light switch multiple times, I had to do it irrespective of where I was. Of course, it was only necessary for thwarting the national vampires. Not all British and French nationals were vampires. Guiding forces and voices would identify the danger immediately and illuminate the angels of darkness.

There were many attractive women in the office but I was resolute in my marriage, despite it slowly falling apart. I had many opportunities to be unfaithful with intoxicating aromas, heightened sexual energy and arousal and an organisational position of status which would have made it easy for me to stray. I just about resisted, though.

Six

There are many myths about people who suffer from psychosis, one of which is implied in the question, 'How many psychotic episodes have you had?' The answer for me was one prolonged psychosis with manic-depressive highs and lows. Once your disease is progressed you are for all purposes clinically insane. There is no normality as such. You just react and respond differently to different situations from day to day. The voices that I heard inside my head were clearly identifiable and did not scare me. They were guiding me through my journey and assisting me in navigating to destinations and making my world colourful with rich aromas, thoughts and sounds. They were sometimes humorous and sometimes deliberate and at times debilitating.

Unfortunately, retrospective analysis is all you are left with after you have been diagnosed. There is no way of knowing when the lines between insanity and reality became blurred. You can only piece together your past thought processes and logically conclude where things just went haywire. If you persist on this train of thought it will lead to frustration and melancholy. Go forward. Just go forward!

Work was becoming virtually impossible for me, as my now severe mood changes were being noticed. I also felt closed in and did not really wish to continue with my employer. It was stopping me expanding and branching out further on my own. All the time I believed that I was being monitored and followed at work and at home. What to do next? Let's take out a mortgage on an apartment in London.

We were tired of paying rent and my wife and I decided

to buy an apartment, with a little help from the banking fraternity. She was working at an upmarket London hotel in the West End and I had a high-paying job. We had paid off multiple mortgages back home and this would be easy. Despite the fact that we were only in London for a two-year secondment, we agreed and proceeded to purchase a property in Islington. It was within walking distance of Angel tube station and as an upcoming area it was rich in cafés, bars and restaurants. Once we left London we would just sell the apartment.

The catalyst for the move was the alarm incident during our Chalk Farm stay. I had returned to our rental home earlier than my wife one night and had forgotten the central alarm code. To complicate events there was an electricity blackout which I believed was due to the ferocious energy emanating from my brain, as it clashed with the Greater London power grid. The alarm went off quite loudly for what seemed to be an eternity and my wife was not picking up her work phone, despite multiple mobile calls. Many residents attended the scene and we were left with no option but to sever the internal wiring. That did not disable the alarm as it continued to ring out into the *cold* London night. The shrieking annoyed me to no end and I felt extremely disappointed that I could not recall the stupid PIN of that damn device. What to do next? I literally hacked the external ringer by using a stepladder, supplied by one of the complaining residents. OK, so time to vacate Chalk Farm. The area was fun whilst it lasted but this was a sign that we should move away and never return. I had severed ties with Chalk Farm as I pondered my next adventure. Our Swiss-French real estate agent did not charge us for the alarm.

So we moved into the borough of Islington, courtesy of HSBC Midland Bank. The banker was exceptionally accommodating and assisted us by circumventing much of the bureaucracy associated with foreign ownership of UK title. This bureaucracy included the section in the loan application which asked if I had ever taken illicit drugs. I left it blank and the banker did not force the issue.

Somehow news travelled to my office that I had purchased a property in central London and the young local executives of similar age were still renting. They were outraged that a foreigner had come to own a part of England before they had. It did not affect me, though, and my wife and I set about renovating with new carpet, new kitchen, new bathroom and washer/dryer. We purchased some furniture and made it our home, never realising that it would witness the cacophonic ramblings of madness. If only those walls could speak, they would recount the graphic story of mind decay and the destruction of innocence.

On our return to our Islington flat from a nightly excursion into the city, I sensed the presence of another person in our apartment as I neared the front door. Armed only with an umbrella, I opened the door slowly and searched throughout the whole apartment, including the closets, to locate the intruder. There was, of course, no one there.

This paranoiac effect was also apparent during our home renovations. Tradespeople would leave their tool bags in our kitchen at the end of the day's work. I strongly believed that their work gear contained microphones and that all the world, through some sort of channel or portal, could access my conversations. Of course I played up for the microphone and made the routine conversations between myself and my wife more engaging. As most of the world was listening, I leant toward exhibitionism and sparked up conversation threads.

This sensation of being constantly followed and monitored would reside with me for a very long time. It was more than paranoia. It was as if my every action and reaction was being scrutinised by a representative board of appointed authorities. Nameless, faceless powers who were documenting my life in preparation for judgement day. How would I fare, though? Would I pass the examination? Would I be catapulted into Herculean status? What did it all mean? When would it end? That was the dilemma. When would the madness end?

The distant light was my only hope. It would all end up fine; I just had to hold on and soldier on and move toward the light, traversing illuminated landscapes and guided by the angelic voices in my head. Yet the demonic voices were also there and would sometimes have their way with my mind. It was this constant battle surging inside and around me that was most crippling. Every day there would be incidental analysis of that day's events. I had to justify all of my actions and reactions to the voices in my head and heed or disobey instruction based on psychotic logic. This would range from which brand of shampoo to purchase to which location to visit next. It did not stop and even whilst dreaming I had to piece together the ever-growing jigsaw puzzle of my life.

The situations were also getting weirder and even more absurd as time progressed. In particular there was an extraordinary encounter involving a tradesman who was painting the inner walls of our apartment. We would leave him a copy of the keys because he plied his trade whilst we were at our respective jobs. Although my wife had selected him to complete the job because he was young and cool, she later came to detest him and they would argue constantly regarding the quality of the work at the end of a day's shift. One night, after he had left, my spouse found her moisturiser bottle opened and believed that he had been using it. So I called him and asked him if he had been using it. It was an unusual accusation and he denied it vehemently. It took for ever for him to complete the work as he was consistently patching over bumps and re-sanding to meet my wife's high standards of completion. Of course, my wife thought that I was an idiot for even mentioning the moisturiser incident to him. I am sure she was after an excuse to cull his services. In any event he finished the work and we paid him in full. He called me 'Governor' and the endorsement sat well with me. I would never see him again, nor did I wish to.

Years later, when I was hypomanic and applying for positions within the banking industry, my job demands would include a year's supply of moisturiser as part of my proposed salary package. Needless to say I would never enter UK banking, nor would my exorbitant demands be met by any employer.

I struck up a friendship with another one of the trades-people working on our home. He was British through and through and would cut me slack on some of the refurbish-ment costs. Yes, he was a good man. I found out that he played guitar and we would chat about our favourite axemen whilst he was working. I determined from our conversations that his personality profile was stronger than mine. I would telepathically reach out to him during my challenging periods and his welcoming replies helped me out during some of those dark moments. The mental call-and-answer exchanges were altogether soothing and it was nice to know that I was not alone. I indeed had friends – sort of – *out there*. His carpentry refurbishments were complete and I would never see him again. Ultimately, that was the way I preferred it then. They had to be chance encounters that passed into the ether, never to be revisited. I craved a different exchange every day and did not want anything holding me back. I needed to isolate all emotional attachment to people and this was another unfulfilled potential friendship.

By this stage, I was not only insane but a threat to myself, my wife and anybody in the immediate vicinity. I remember my wife angered me over something trivial and I slapped her hard across the cheek. This happened twice. I did not know what had come over me. Some other power had taken hold of me. It was not in my nature as I was and am fairly logical and keep emotions in check. This does not necessarily mean bottled up. It just means that I keep my cool under normal circumstances. I was falling completely off the edge of the known world and transcending into some other world, which, in reality, I had created in my own mind.

Being conscious of having dropped out of an 'A-grade' university back home, I tried to gain entry into the London Business School for executive study. So I called the faculty and spoke to a dean. I outlined my request and he asked me my national background. I advised him, 'I carry a Hellenic passport.' He picked up on the metaphor that, of course, I carried a Hellenic Republic. He was not amused and replied, 'So you are Greek!' We argued via emailed correspondence and jointly decided against entry into the school. I settled on the University of London. They were more welcoming, less intrusive and more aligned to my requirements.

This desire to complete an advanced degree plagued me for a long time and I would eventually become obsessed with the idea. In my mind, as long as I continued with my quest, any prior academic shortcomings would be forgiven by 'the system' and *they* would allow me passage into the real UK world. The world where I would be accepted. I am not and have never been a social climber, but for those unfamiliar with London, or the UK for that matter, you need to settle on your area of fulfilment. This could be artistic, creative, social or business-oriented. Failure to do so will result in continuous drifting and you will be lost forever. The amusing happy London postcards you send back during a holiday do not tell the whole story.

Plagued by the presence of Oxbridge graduates, I wished to shine ever so brightly and not be dragged down by the burden of unqualified work experience. I felt obligated to be the best I could be, and to achieve this I needed to dominate boardrooms and classrooms. I would find a way! Or, as one of my London colleagues aptly summed up, 'You are intelligent. You need to find solutions to problems and not break the door down.' How could he be so right? His observations were correct. I would always think my way through challenges and I would avoid conflict by circumventing obstacles.

My plight was being played out literally and metaphorically on television also. I witnessed an interview with an Oxford professor stating that sometimes being happy, not just achievements, is what fulfilment is all about. The pursuit of happiness will release you from the cycle you create for yourself. I knew he was referring to me and he was right. I was searching for happiness which I could not find anywhere. His comments were true. I cried myself uncontrollably to sleep that night. In fact his comments spun an obsessive web in my mind as I searched for answers to enlightenment and contentment.

Whilst I was having these delusional thoughts, and interacting with every other person, including my wife, on an irrational basis, I still had the feeling that I was continually being monitored and followed. The night I cried uncontrollably, I caught a glimpse of a teddy bear which my wife had purchased to decorate the house. I was convinced there was a camera in one of its eyes, so I turned its head around so that it would face away from me. In print media the next day I saw a corporation advertisement showing somebody ripping off a teddy bear's head, stating words to the effect of 'time to make a switch'. Teddy did not stand a chance and would live out his life looking out of our lounge window. My wife would switch him back to his normal position every so often until she gave up on my teddy reversal obsession. It was as if this corporation was reaching out to me in my time of need and validating my need for expressive freedom. It was great to know I was not alone.

My wife and I would attend parties and dinners with my wife's co-workers. There were plenty of women and their intoxicating aromas were driving me sexually insane. I was getting flirtatious and dangerous, even when in close proximity to my wife, but each time I resisted my urges. I remember one trip to Wales where I asked my wife if I could have an affair. She said, 'Don't ask me!' Was I supposed to go ahead and just have a fling with someone? I was uncontrollably insatiable with a ferocious sexual appetite. My wife would just about keep up with my demands. I could not get enough!

I recall attending a cinema screening one night in Notting Hill. My wife and I sat next to each other. My wife was on my right. On my left was a beautiful woman whose face I did not gaze upon. From my peripheral vision I made out that she was wearing a sky-blue top. As the movie swung into gear I could smell her scent and it was heavenly. The smell illuminated like a light. I let my senses go and found both our scents merged into one. Despite the lack of physical contact it was still a very erotic experience and I wanted the movie to last forever. I did not gaze upon her. It was more romantic without making eye contact. As if by design, an accidental brush of her arm with my hand, as I changed positions in my seat, adrenalised me spectacularly. Still I resisted looking into her eyes. I was tempted, though. My God, was I tempted, but it would have circumvented a beautiful moment. I will never forget that smell. It was amazing! Woman!

For a bipolar sufferer hallucinations are not restricted to the auditory and visual senses. Your sense of smell is also affected as you believe you are soaking in aromas which do not actually exist. In my case they were aromas linked to people that I knew. Therefore, when in some European city I would smell the scent of old girlfriends and could clearly identify which scent belonged where. If nothing else it made my travels more fun and linked my story from early childhood to that point in time. It all came together as I pieced together the disjointed jigsaw of my life.

Seven

Toward the end of my stint with my employer, I was shifting between mania, hypomania and depression quite rapidly. During one client visit, I was walking toward Liverpool Street tube station after just leaving the central London office. There were some colleagues walking toward me in the opposite direction. One of those colleagues was a young lady carrying an umbrella. Without warning I grabbed the umbrella from her in one motion and continued walking. My colleagues continued toward work in the opposite direction and did not react to my action. Full of rage and with umbrella in hand I headed toward the tube station. As I reached the entry gate I parted both my arms, still holding the umbrella, and exploded into life. I felt the full force of my will and for that moment in time I had achieved nirvana at that exact location. It was beyond elation. It was, and I was, absolute. I wished to be closer to God. I wished to be one with God. For a brief passage in time, I was God. Nobody dared lock gaze with me. I must have scared a lot of people at the time. This was an episode of fully blown mania. I carried the umbrella up the elevator and left the article at our client's premises at the conclusion of our meeting. I was now 'covering' the client with my reach. I would never use the left entry gate of Liverpool Street station again.

Weekend trips were frequent and also included multiple trips to Belgium, France and Italy. I was gaining momentum and increasing my international aspirations, but I was completely out of control.

During one of those weekends away, we headed off to Belgium, the people of which in my Euro mind-mapping were 'killers'. The sort of people who end all fun and frivolity based on a quick ending to entertainment, or so I thought. Whilst in Brussels, I remember having telepathic communication with someone I had known from my home. Feeling like he was overpowering me, I decided to act savagely. I mentally acquired a samurai sword and decapitated him with one violent striking motion. All this occurred in my mind and I felt empowered by this act of defiance. It calmed me down and cleared my mind and thoughts temporarily.

Deciding that Belgium was the best place to discard my work ID card, I tossed it into a nearby bin at the airport. I was free at last. The actual act of throwing out the employee ID card relieved some stress in my mind and released some mental toxicity. I believed that the poison infiltrating my mind was connected to the actual identification card and possession of it. Sweet endorphins were released as I completed another international transaction!

That Monday the office door was wide open. The receptionist was smiling. It was as if the path into the office was illuminated. It was a brighter day than normal for overcast London. I thought that the office had welcomed my ritual and I was both happy and relieved. Not quite. It was a malfunction which had disabled the security system. I had to bother other employees to lend me their work ID cards when I wanted to go to the bathroom. Eventually I tired of the whole thing and simply resigned in a messy fall-out with the management team some days later.

The day before the resignation I had arranged for some one-on-one time with the managing director. I wanted to discuss what I believed was the microscopic and unappreciated pursuit of personal information pertaining to myself. The managing director was coincidentally, or maybe even conveniently, absent on the day of our scheduled meeting. This unnerved me, but I did not dare show any weakness. In my mind he did not wish to be part of the carnage that would be the resignation fall-out. He did not wish to witness blood.

It was a heated exchange. The HR director and my one-up stated that I had agreed on a two-year deal and was basically reneging and walking out before the end of the agreed timeframe. I stared them both down defiantly and summoned all of my inner strength to walk out with no one in the office engaging me. I succeeded. I walked out mighty and tall. All of the other employees were buried in their PCs, pretending to be working. The look on my face would have been frightening and nobody dared to approach me.

I made my way back to my Islington flat to explain to my wife that I had just resigned. When she arrived from her workplace she seemed to take it all in her stride, stating that I would find another employer very quickly.

So why did I resign? There were psychotic mitigating circumstances associated with the lead-up to the resignation. My one-up working-class line manager kept on referring to the mood as 'greasy' around the office. I interpreted this as the mood lacking the automatically lubricated feel of Greece. In order for me to lead the office environment into a fully functioning unit I needed to apply the right amount of grease (Greece). To achieve this I had to cast my presence across the whole organisation. To solidify the experience I had to leave. I was the gap between dysfunction and automation. My physical presence was slowing down the system. Not quite martyrdom, but I needed to evacuate the environment to ensure continuity and efficiencies were introduced and maintained. My departure would complete the fluidity. It was the only logical way! I reasoned telepathically with the marketing manager and we both agreed that it was indeed the only way to resolve the situation.

I tried to find other work immediately, but I was steamrolled by depression. Believing that my destiny would be financially rewarding, I had lost all concept of loans and savings.

At this point I need to stress the difference between feeling depressed and clinical depression. As a diagnosed manic-depressive I can report first-hand that clinical depression is exceptionally dangerous. I literally could not get out of bed. I felt a massive weight burden me for no reason. I could not physically, let alone mentally, function as other people could. I also lost all appetite and subsequently lost weight. I remember I thought that I had contracted some physical ailment. There was nothing physically wrong with me. It was full-on depression. The days and nights melted into each other and my marriage was practically over. Darkness fell upon me and demons ran riot inside my now fragile, vulnerable mind. They were literally taking over my existence. I thought that this state would be my future for ever. I did not believe that I would ever break free of their grasp.

I began to feel paranoid about my health, so I contacted the local general practitioner regarding setting up an urgent appointment. They could not oblige my desperate plea. In an explosive fit of rage I blasted them and slammed the phone down and bounced it off its switch-hook without disconnecting the call. The practice had not hung up. That was good enough for me. I knew then and there that the British health system would not forsake me.

I asked about insurance cover and the practice stated that it would be a good idea to obtain some. So I contacted Bupa as I believed they were the only truly *caring* organisation in their field. In fact, during my interview for the London job I remember asking about health insurance and the employer mentioned that they had an agreement in place with Bupa; however, we did not lock down the 'cover' in my salary deal.

Bupa provided me with a ten-digit account number over the phone, which I still remember to this day. I felt relief knowing that I was 'covered'. I hid the account number somewhere in the apartment furniture and committed it to memory until the end of time. I have never paid Bupa for any health services and I am still a bit confused as to how I was able to register an account with them.

I was now certifiably indestructible and had a back-up guardian in case of emergency. This constituted immortality in my mind and I would forever see Bupa advertisements illuminated against the backdrop of other signage. They would resurrect me on my darker, moodier days.

Relieved that the English nation would carry my ever-increasing 'workload', I decided to pamper myself. I had been experiencing residual back pain from depression and complained about this to my wife. She advised me to seek a massage, so I did. I telephoned multiple listed massage therapists to assist with the stifling pressure mounting in my lower back. I settled on an inner-city London massage parlour.

I must have been carrying a valid underground travel ticket as I recall only carrying a £10 note in my pocket. I fronted up to the establishment and was greeted by an exceptionally friendly male receptionist. He was delighted to see me and shook my hand continuously. It seemed a little odd at the time but I did not think too much about it. Business must have been slow. I waited for a few minutes before he led me to a room with a massage table on it.

A woman appeared in a nurse's uniform with a dangerously lowly applied zip. She had jet-black hair, black eyes and a stunning figure and was defiant as she exposed her bubbly cleavage. Her outfit barely left anything to a man's imagination as it was virtually in line with her underwear. She asked me to strip completely and so I did. She performed a massage and asked me for money. I handed her the ten pounds. She asked curiously, 'You came for a massage, yeah?' I replied, 'Yes.' She then stated that a tenner did not buy much here. She snatched the banknote, though. Business really must have been slow that day or she was in a frisky mood that afternoon. She gratified me and relieved me of all my tension. As we were completing our affair I raised my forehead to kiss her. She almost accepted the offer, but at the last moment hesitated and declined politely by saying, 'I would love to but we are not allowed to.' Her scent was of pure sex and I felt it on myself that whole afternoon and well into the night.

When I returned to the flat my wife asked me if I had received a massage. I stated, 'Yes.'

Later on that week my wife had planned a dinner for the two of us. It had been on the agenda for some time and my wife had built up the event for a while now. I was led to believe that we were going to dine at a new restaurant in Covent Garden. This had been the agreed plan some nights earlier. As we were departing, and as if she knew that the house was bugged, she put her index finger to my lip and hushed me.

We ventured out to a restaurant in Islington. It was like a mystical experience. The night was alive and it was as if the restaurant door had opened automatically for us. I looked around and knew that all the people dining were attendees in my soon-to-be-revealed theatrical performance. I subtly acknowledged their presence. I looked toward a man I thought was a Greek banker and his wife. He shook his head in disapproval. They would not grant me passage into the Greek banking industry. I was too controversial a figure.

My wife was asking me weird questions about my thoughts on life, business and politics. There was a middle-aged English couple nearby. They were pretend-ing not to listen. I was boasting how Diego Maradona's goal against England in the 1986 World Cup was more than the greatest goal ever scored. It was vindication for Argentina over the Falklands War. It carried the Argentine nation and was sweet and defiant in the player's poetic disablement of the English defence. I went on and on all night and felt pokes and prods in the couch every time I zoned out due to my depression. I continued to recall instances of when the British would do anything to avoid a black mark against their record, such as an infringement notice or anything that would blemish their bureaucratic nature and profile. I was in full flight. After all, I was being interviewed by my wife for my next challenge, which was passage into mainstream English life and acceptance as the chosen one.

That night I fell into a deep slumber until I was awoken by a force which picked me up and manoeuvred me to the telephone to call my uncle in Greece. We had maintained telephone contact and he had asked me to call him at a particular time on a particular day. I had forgotten all about it. Controlling forces had not forgotten.

Those few minutes felt dream-like and confusing. I was literally not in control of my movement, but was not afraid. My uncle was delighted to hear my voice, as was I to hear his. The fact that I had succeeded in meeting my obligation re-invigorated me momentarily. I was still slipping further and further into morbid depression and this would cripple me physically and mentally.

At the time of this severe depression, I recall listening to the *In Utero* CD by Nirvana. I was lost in the songs as I tried to sound out hidden messages. I was lying on the carpet of the bedroom at the time and found their underlying tones hypnotic and mysterious but, alas, they did not pave the way for any answers. Their music, I believed, had not been certified by the Royal Academy of Music, so it was very dangerous to listen to. I recall trying to explain this to my wife. The Academy would only certify certain acts, such as the Beatles (still my favourite band), by endorsing their music as above the required normality threshold. It was OK to listen to them. Nirvana had no endorsement, so their music had mind-altering subtleties. And I was, of course, experimental if nothing else. All the while being stalked and haunted by passages from my own creation, 'Death by Politics':

... Do not look at me, do not even lean on me for support.
You do not know it but I mean to end it all ...

Considerably depressed, I headed off by foot to central London where I locked eyes with a man standing outside a Beatles memorabilia store, beckoning people inside with the obligatory 'magical mystery tour' greeting.

Whilst stopping short of having direct telepathic communication with Sir Paul McCartney, who is still by far my favourite Beatle, I was convinced that I would fall into his mental auspice as a follower, which would alleviate the burden of maintaining momentum with my ever-growing mental database of followers. I ventured into the store as if it had fallen into my path by cosmic forces. The in-store experience did not meet my expectations and, like many other smaller spin-off theories to resolve my immense pain, my conviction did not eventuate into reality. For some reason I could not make that magical mental connection with Sir Paul. I resolved this in my mind as the both of us maintaining our own spiritual identities without any overlap possible. Let it be!

Still uncontrollably depressed and feeling forsaken, I was flirting with the idea of time travel and convinced myself that it was indeed possible. It had started with a fleeting thought when I was living in our marital home and developed into pure obsession. I believed that I could cast my presence into some point in time and whilst I may have aged or changed that place would remain forever the same. I could travel through various time periods without disturbing the different virtualisations I had created. This would be repeated predominantly in Paris, where I would return to the same Left Bank hotel only to find it had the same look and feel as when I had left it many times before. I was now controlling time. I was indeed a Time Lord!

The only place where I could not control time was Switzerland. There seemed to be a gap to allow for Swiss control of overall time. They were the time overlords and would leave a valley between places and images to ensure that the universe could breathe. Believing this to be true, I headed off to the local library and pored over historic references with respect to post-World-War-II Switzerland. My research turned up, of course, the well-documented conspiracy theories surrounding the Swiss and the amassed fortunes they acquired at the end of the Second World War. My Swiss-French friend would more often than not show her French side (her mother's side). This made me happier considering what I thought I knew about Switzerland!

I was still incredibly depressed and inconsolable as I could not find a job. Whilst looking for employment I stumbled on a telephone number given to me by one of my business associates from home. He had been a client of mine and had told me that his mother was staying with her partner in Surrey, England. He had provided me with her details during a farewell dinner we had arranged prior to my wife and me heading off to the UK.

On the way to Surrey my wife and I stopped to purchase a dinner gift. I settled on a large chocolate cello. It seemed cute and appropriate. When we arrived, after much asking of directions, the four of us started laughing when, to our surprise, there was a classical cello solo on the sound system. We weren't sure who had 'pinned' whom first. Let's call it a draw.

I would always recite a song in my head to power up for meetings, and this was no exception.

We had a lovely time! I advised them that I was looking for employment as I knew they were recruitment consultants in my field. The lady's partner advised me to keep going and not to stop. It was like he knew that I needed to show *them* strength through adversity. I would never see them again despite having regular post-dinner telephone and email communication. They were a nice couple. I didn't deliberately try to 'pin' them.

I would later catch up with my business associate whilst residing at my parents' home and recount the catch-up with his mother and her partner to him. I did not mention the cello incident.

My client was a great person, and I remember my wife and me having dinner with him and his girlfriend in his very nice apartment not far from our marital home. We would also dine out in upmarket restaurants together. During one dinner sitting, and only weeks before departing for London, I was trying to explain the behavioural differences between London and New York City to my wife and this couple. London, I stated, would develop a form of 'in vogue' behaviour, but it was New York City which would actually make it happen. In essence, Londoners would invent the behavioural trait and New Yorkers would run with it.

My client asked me if I was just an operator or the real deal. I am still not quite sure what he meant at the time, but made sense of his comment as recognition of my ever-increasing brand. I would make it happen in London and eventually spread it throughout New York and the rest of the world. The quickening had stirred inside me. It was at that particular time, at that particular restaurant, that I was awoken from my passive existence and decided then and there that my time was about to come and I would explode into vitality. The waiter accidentally smashed a glass and I felt the inadvertent act provide me with the distraction I required. Suddenly, the colours of the food and the backdrop of the restaurant were clearer and brighter than ever before. I knew then that it was now my time on planet Earth.

Music would play a major part in my journey as I constantly found myself searching for new ideas and new streams of information. In fact, one day I traded my whole CD collection for a few classical CDs. The same CDs I had held the grudge over so many years ago. I also disposed of any copyright-infringing CDs. After all, I needed to be clean to enter into British society. I admitted to myself that I had made careless *mistakes* in the past, but now I was crystal clear.

I would also interpret cryptic messages from the MTV music channel during my global adventure. The television hosts would carefully issue warnings regarding the forces of evil's impending capture of my mind and the systematic normalisation of my existence. Only I could decipher these touch points and carry out the hosts' instructions. I dared not reveal them to anyone at all. I would protect them and their message, the same way that they were protecting me. They would subtly inform me of approaching danger and the applicable outs. I would heed their advice and interpret the clues by toeing the global minefield.

Eight

As our marriage was dissolving I recall one night where I flew into an utter fit of rage. My wife had annoyed me with some trivial comment she had made about something even more trivial. I was yelling and screaming at her like a madman in my loudest possible voice. I am sure that all the neighbours heard the whole tirade. In any event, in a fearful state close to sheer panic she locked herself in the bathroom. I immediately broke the door down (it was lockable from the inside) and confronted her in a desperate, uncontrollable manner. It was terrifying for both of us, especially for her. This was not my normal behaviour and it came from the depths of insanity. I ranted and raved and verbally attacked her in no uncertain terms. My voice was also foreign to my normal tone and colour and it upset her considerably.

The official end of our marriage and inevitable subsequent separation came after a three-day bender I partook of in Paris. Equipped with the clothes I was wearing and a credit card, I left my wife a hand-written note stating that I would be back in a few days. She was still actively employed and I left during her business hours.

I arrived at Paris airport in a state of hypomania. Carrying an EU passport I slipped past customs with relative ease. My Air France boarding pass was housed in my passport. I dropped this at customs as a mental claim that I had conquered the UK and was now going to conquer France. I was inches away from yelling out, 'Liberté, égalité, fraternité!' The vibe in the French airport was electric. I still love Paris, but I loved it even more then.

I had been to Paris many times and so headed off to the Left Bank. My view of the street lights was uncluttered and the vibrant colours against the museum background were magnificent. I believed that I had heightened visual perception, despite wearing glasses, and could see magic as if peering through a kaleidoscope. The whole city exploded with colour and warmth, and I was loving it.

After exiting the Parisian taxi with no luggage, my first concern was accommodation. As the portal access into my life was well documented, governing powers would be compensating me financially for violating my personal information database and making it publically available. Money was no obstacle. I was accelerating in the globalisation of my personal brand and millions would be pouring in from some sort of massive financial deal.

I checked into a five-star Parisian hotel. It was magnificent. I entered my room, took off my top and admired my torso in the mirror. I was still wearing my black designer jeans. I then allowed myself mentally, physically and metaphysically to release the UK atmosphere and be absorbed by the known Parisian thought processes. As I gazed into the mirror I felt transformed. My eyes had a French look about them and were markedly different to my UK gaze. I became French. Welcome to Paris, sir!

I rested for a little while and then walked out into the oncoming Paris streets. I was hypomanic and loving every minute of it. I was in need of a toothbrush, so I popped into a chemist and purchased one. It is amazing to think that even during my most insane periods personal hygiene was always paramount in my mind.

Being European in background I passed easily as a local as I ordered take-out coffee. I walked endlessly for long periods of time, stopping periodically to eat and jump on and off the Metro train system. I travelled all over Paris and mind-mapped the landscape. I was going to 'protect Paris' because I was superhuman and anywhere that I graced with my presence would fall under my auspice as 'controlled longitude and latitude'. I tried not to suffocate the city and allowed multiple exits for creativity via multiple Gare du Nord exits.

I would frequent laundrettes to wash and dry my underwear and would purchase different tops. During one visit to a laundrette I heard a gunshot, but in my hypomanic state I was not afraid, because I had transcended all fear boundaries. I was, after all, invincible! The gunshot was meant for me! My Swiss-French friend was protecting me and as always I felt her guiding presence watching over me.

I ended up at the museum, where I was greeted by a subdued French museum employee. The employee was frail and had a lean outline. He asked me to pay the entrance fee. I asked him if he was sure he wanted to ask me that. He cowered and let his shoulders slump. I overpowered my way into the museum and marvelled at the art. It was a glorious day and I was captivated by the beauty I was beholding. Upon departing the museum I threw a strong defiant glance at the employee. He looked away.

Continuing my Paris field trip, I ended up at the French Bourse. I accepted the tour which was in the French language. I could not understand a single word, but they seemed to believe I was French. I could travel Europe and take the national identity of each country I was visiting. Globalisation with local presence and local thought! I was moving effortlessly and swiftly, adjusting direction according to the instruction in my head. It was absolute bliss. I was totally free, without a care in the world, and was camouflaging myself well within my European surroundings.

I did, however, have to apologise to a Japanese businessman staying at the same hotel as me. Allow me to explain. Upon my arrival on a previous bender, there had been a group of Japanese tourists in the lift with me. They had given me priority exit as the lift had opened in another expensive hotel somewhere in Euroland. I had commented to the local hotel staff employee, 'Polite, aren't they?' Upon my arrival back in London at Heathrow, there had been another group of Japanese tourists ahead of me. The airport officer had said something, which I thought was, 'Polite, aren't they?' I assumed that my communication had transcended the international airwaves and that everyone had heard my previous comment.

So I was now at the bar of the French hotel where an upset Japanese businessman was gazing at me, seeking explanation for my comment. I telepathically communicated that it was a simple comment and by no means did I mean to show disrespect. His frown turned to a smile and he scrunched up the French invoice and said to the bartender, 'Take it. It is rubbish.' In my mind I had created the Greco-Japanese alliance by this one act of sincerity. Japan was on side! The world would be mine – very soon.

The French hotel was my sanctuary and I could return to it after an extensive rebuilding, in my mind, of the French capital city.

I had expected the French people to throw open their arms to me and embrace me as one of their own. In my mind they did not. After a few days I was bored of my little trip and decided to return to London. I arrived at the airport and purchased a ticket on the next available flight to Heathrow.

Upon returning to London, I entered our Islington apartment to find my wife in tears. I had been gone for three days and fifty-one minutes. 'Where have you been?' she asked.

I just shrugged my shoulders and said, 'Paris.' I advised her that our relationship was over because it was not working out. We lived together for the next six weeks or so, before she moved out with one of her girlfriends.

I clearly recall the night of our marriage dissolution. I stated in a teary tone that she still had a husband who loved her very much but that we could not continue on like this. She was also crying but did not grant my request for a friendly hug. We were both visibly upset. It was like a death in the family. I was on a global mission, though, and I felt that the relationship was stifling me, plus the fact that we were constantly arguing – mainly because I was insane and had no logical reason for any of my actions. If I had not been psychotic, would the relationship have blossomed into something beautiful? Maybe. It is hard to say. Would we have carried the same attraction if I had not been insane? You need to remember that I was well on the way to insanity on our fateful wedding day. The circumstances were what they were and even the sacrament of marriage, witnessed by God in his place of worship, could be broken by man.

Our wedding day was quite nice too! We had two services, one Catholic and one Orthodox. My wife walked to her local parish from her parents' home with all the bridesmaids. This was her childhood wish. We then headed over to the Orthodox church for a service at my parish. The reception was great and we checked into an expensive inner-city hotel for the night, before flying out the next morning to Los Angeles en route to our American honeymoon. Someone had passed me a marijuana joint that night, which I accepted and finished off as my wife was changing out of her wedding dress. It was a very romantic night which lasted, because I was unnaturally high, a very, very long time!

During those six weeks after my return from Paris I was in a state of mania. I took a trip to Nice for no apparent reason. I remember I flew to Paris and made my way to the French Riviera. Arriving in Nice, I made my way to the city centre by way of local taxi. It must have been close to midnight and I was totally alive and wired.

After exiting the cab, I walked down the main street, as unknown powers guided me in my travel. Turning left and right was dependent on where commanding powers would allow me to navigate to. The correct path would be illuminated against the southern Mediterranean backdrop. It was a very warm night. I ended up at the entrance of an amazing hotel and asked for a reservation in my name. There was no reservation, so I handed over my credit card and checked into my paid-for room.

The next day I awoke refreshed, invigorated and full of life. I visited the hotel swimming pool surrounded by European wealth and aristocracy, overlooking the sea. It was magnificent.

I ordered a toasted chicken focaccia and it was served to me slightly burnt. I was in internal conflict as to whether to return it or not. In my mind I was being tested for passage into European royalty and had to either eat the chicken focaccia or have it returned. I was also very hungry. I answered the voices in my head by stating to them that it was irrelevant whether I returned the meal or not. It did not mean that I had failed the test, because I was, after all, extremely hungry, and I was also not impressed by being tested in this manner. This was because all along during my disease I was against personal information becoming public. I stood up for personal freedom. But I needed to eat. I was Rousseau's noble savage.

Later in that day, clutching a letter from my credit card company's UK office, I switched on the television and watched the cable news channel. My publically listed credit card company would shortly be announcing their results. Forecasts were not looking promising. They had been hounding me to refer their brand to as many people as I could. I would not comply and was now going head-to-head with the financial institution.

I left Paris and headed for Athens to complete the disruptive transaction. Having checked into an expensive hotel room, I ran a warm bath and contemplated what to do next. Believing that all reliance and addictions had to be broken, I tore up the credit card company's referral letter and cut up the credit card into tiny pieces. The hotel staff had previously obliged my request with a pair of sharp scissors. I flushed the pieces down the toilet within the stylishly modern bathroom. A layer of concern was lifted or rather stripped from my exposed subconscious. I lay in the warm bath and waited for nature to take its course.

I switched on the television and tuned in to a financial news channel. The company had taken a massive hit and the stock had been sent plummeting. Let that be a warning to other brands trying to ride my journey. I was not going to sell my soul. Financial endorsements needed to be provided to me with no obligation. I was not going to become a corporate slave.

It was warm in Athens that day, so I celebrated solitarily with ouzo, basking in the nice weather. I had carried the referral letter across Europe for at least two months. I did not pay for the ouzo. The establishment did not ask for any money.

Another day, another trip. This time to Geneva, Switzerland, where my Swiss-French friend had returned after her time in London. She was fed up with London and Geneva was her home town. She had landed a marketing position in a medium-sized Swiss organisation.

I arrived at the airport and checked into a very expensive hotel, despite the tourist information desk insisting that I stay at a cheaper complex. Upon entering my lavish hotel room, I called the Swisscom operator and asked for my friend's telephone details. She was listed. Words could not quite capture my emotions and feelings at that point in time. I called my Swiss-French lady friend nervously and she answered. I was elated. I identified myself and she stated that she was single. We agreed to catch up later that afternoon after she had finished working. She would pick me up from my hotel, at an agreed time, and we would see the sights of Geneva together.

I spent the remainder of the day writing letters in a very posh and expensive café and sending them to people and organisations I 'knew'. They were nonsensical and I am not sure what the whole purpose was. The letters were written on premier parched paper which I had purchased from a nearby store. I tried to make my handwriting as classically scripted as possible. Do not ask me to whom they were addressed. I just remember the nice weather and feeling totally relaxed in Geneva. A Swiss-French angel was guiding and guarding me! I do remember affixing stamps on them, though.

I started getting bored and would eventually run out of time-consuming ideas, as I ventured across those Geneva cobblestone paths. I headed off to the local branch of the Credit Suisse bank. I entered the bank conscious of the satellite tracking device attached to my prescription lenses, which was relaying information to *them*. I asked for access to a considerable Swiss bank account in my name. After handing over my Hellenic passport to the bank employee, I learnt, to my surprise, there was no such bank account. I asked her to check again. She did not oblige. I would also re-enact the whole process at multiple English banking branches with always the same result. Where and when was my big pay day going to occur? Should I keep receipts of my travel? If I did keep receipts, where would I store them? Some person or thing needed to lift my burden and pick up my trail and financially liberate me.

I even remember on one occasion approaching the teller of my local Islington bank for a withdrawal from this supposed monster account. She asked me for my passport and bank card. I handed them over simultaneously and they dropped from my outstretched hand and landed on the tray below. As they fell, they bounced *strategically* and the card landed on the tray first with the Hellenic passport landing on top. Accidental? Perhaps. I read more into it, as did the bank employee who brandished a warm smile as our eyes *accidentally* met. The imagery was beautiful. Greece was covering British banking? Greece was under-writing British banking?

In any case, my Swiss-French friend arrived in a fairly ordinary vehicle, disembarked, kissed me twice on the cheek and we headed off together in her car. She and I ended up having a few drinks and a light meal somewhere. I also checked out of the hotel I was staying at as she found me a 'nicer' hotel near her apartment and close to her favourite Protestant church. I would visit her church and light a candle so that we could bond spiritually under a heavenly witness. It was a beautiful moment.

I am not sure if it was before or after our café visit that she invited me to her apartment. I entered with her and she left me alone in the main lounge room, whilst she changed outfits. She returned shortly thereafter and she approached me to the point where we were in very close physical proximity. She ventured closer and I could sense her deep breathing and her sexual presence. Her aroma was heavenly. Was I supposed to make a move? I still felt trapped by my marriage, which for all intents and purposes had ended only a short time before. The moment in time passed quickly and yet I still recall her enduring scent.

That night I returned to my hotel room and called her multiple times as I was feeling uncontrollably elated and euphoric. I deposited a letter in her mailbox stating, *See you in London ASAP*, and the next day I returned to London. She did not reciprocate. I was devastated!

Off to Paris and Athens again, and so on and so on. I was spreading my wingspan across multiple European cities. Each time I would choose different airlines so that they could all receive my blessing for safe air time. At this stage I perceived myself to be a global peace crusader fighting 'controlling powers' and trying to spread as much joy and love as possible. I would also leave a trail of discarded possessions on each flight. These possessions would range from musical listening devices to stationery and of course the scribbled writings of some passing revelation. Each object would be carefully and strategically placed based upon the latest provocation of the forces controlling my every movement. Each time I would transact in this way it would release a calming endorphin representative of the abandonment of another layer of toxic materialism. It was very liberating and I could literally feel the burden of the object brand lifting with each discard. Perfect resonance in a world which I had created full of cluttered dissonance!

During every journey I would take on the national profile of the airline. I would fly Italian, German, French, Austrian, Dutch and many other airlines, changing my section preference at random. I believed that I could morph into any identity and slip by as a national of that airline. It was empowering and exciting. I would seldom take out insurance as I believed I was much stronger than any airline and that they could only benefit from my presence and blessing. I would even flirt with the stewardesses, telling them cryptic stories of my greatness, which would soon be revealed to the world. I would speak in riddles and outline even more grandiose versions of my state of mind. I felt comfortable in the air as I believed that my thought could freely escape and the international clearance did not restrict me to any country or demarcation point. I was truly godlike, thirty thousand feet in the air.

By this stage, I was controlled by all communication from radio and television and conversations I would overhear in the street. Totally wired, I believed that the forces of good were subtly assisting me against controlling interests. I remember entering the local Islington library and overhearing the librarian say 'France'. The next day I would fly off to Paris upon instruction. I also borrowed the book *Voices from a French Village*. I did not read it. I was finding it hard to concentrate on anything for long periods of time. This continued with no clear rhythm or logic. I was getting off on the sounds of my environment. It was like magic!

I would eventually burn my library card in a hypomanic episode and mail it to the USA embassy closest to my parents' place. I ensured my identification was illegible as the card became disfigured and melted into a pile of plastic lava. Metaphoric representation? Maybe. My complex thought processes made it necessary to destroy anything when I became aware of its game plan. I craved spontaneity! Whilst the library was a sanctuary, it had become overly staged and theatrical in outcome, so I had to defuse its power and my addiction to its sanctity. I stopped going there and by destroying the card had momentarily liberated myself from this cycle of madness.

Returning to the Islington flat was difficult at times because the whole street would become illuminated as if to guide me on the way to my door. Every time I would sense a presence and would enter the flat with trepidation and fear. This went on for a long time, as if I was expecting some force to knock me back into a normal path. I was also hoping and longing for my Swiss-French friend to arrive. I sensed her presence all over Europe.

All across Euroland I would overhear various comments about me and my journey. The references would navigate me through the various countries and also guide me through my travels. One American Midwest accent stated, 'Yes, but it must be a Greek key.' This was obviously referring to a passage from one of my earlier poems outlining how only I had the key and the answer. The American woman must have had access to my collection and was subtly engaging me in passing conversation. I interpreted her comment as frustration because only I was the guardian of the secrets of life. The secrets she must have been looking for.

To compound the connection with my Swiss-French friend I overheard another American lady state, whilst in close proximity to me, 'There must be two of them.' This infuriated me because our love was sacred and the American lady had no right to comment on our telepathic love affair. I quickly dismissed this and other passing comments and continued on my meandering passage.

During a hypomanic period I created theories linking specific universities to specific behaviours and thought patterns. I believed that no Cambridge graduates could start new theories and all of them were trapped in recurring patterns of behaviour based on existing fundamental principles. Whilst I was working in London I had to take a train to a client's premises outside London. I was running late and wished to contact the customer to advise so. I had left my mobile in Islington and had to use a public payphone, but which one? There was a scrunched-up piece of paper on top of one of the payphones. This was a sign. As I picked up the receiver the female station voice announced, 'Cambridge,' in a clear tone. I had cracked the code. The verbalisation's timing was perfect.

Oxford was different, though. I would hire a car many times and head toward the university grounds. However, as I came within a mile or so, I would feel overwhelming power restraining me and find myself unable to proceed. This was because original ideas came from Oxford and it would be too dangerous for my world and the Oxford world to collide. Aside from myself, only Oxford could lay claim to *ego* or *I*. The ability to stand alone.

I was uncovering Britain's greatest secrets and thus becoming a marked man. Controlling forces would wish to halt my journey.

One of those nights, as I was returning from another incomplete trip to Oxford, I recalled a gift from my late teenage years presented to me by two friends of mine. They had just returned from Europe following a university trip which took in London. The gift was an Oxford University T-shirt, emblazoned with the institution's motto: *Dominus Illuminatio Mea* ('the Lord is my light'). One of my friends commented when handing over the top, 'If you cannot attend Oxford University, you may as well have a T-shirt from there.' He meant it in jest, referring to my recent withdrawal from the best university available to all of us.

The night I returned from that Oxford excursion I believed that my friend had known back then about the Oxford syndrome and had been subtly warning me about my future adventures. But how was that possible? I put two and two together and concluded that all of my encountered incidents up to this point were not accidental; my life had been pre-planned from birth. *They* were all part of the conspiracy and my life was not being abstractly constructed but meticulously planned out with deliberate intervention. This infuriated me and I turned the car around and headed back to collide with the university. Again, some incredible force stopped me as I neared the hallowed colleges. It was as if the force was coming from the sky. Heavenly? Not quite, but very eerie.

Nine

A male relative of mine came to stay with me for a week or so. He flew into London from Greece. I had asked him to call me when he arrived so I could pick him up from Angel tube station. He did not call as he wanted to surprise me. Yet I sensed his arrival. Controlling forces summoned me from the lounge and I walked toward the tube without knowing what time or what day he would be arriving. I met him halfway down the street as if by magic.

It was good to see a familiar face. We went out clubbing and partying and I literally prayed for his safe return to his home. He too was recently divorced and we exchanged 'war stories'. I asked him to contact me when his return flight landed so that I knew he was OK. By this stage I believed that anyone who was associated with me would be in grave danger. I was telepathically receiving the OK from the captaining pilot of the flight, as he navigated over the globe. I did not sleep the night that my relative's plane departed.

On another occasion a female relative came to stay with me. I set out to pick her up from the Cambridge rail station. I self-decreed that I would not take directions, but rather utilise the live forces to guide me through the concrete jungle of highways and urban roads. It was increasingly difficult but the voices in my head insisted on using my innate instinct to self-direct to the destination.

Despite my resolve, I had to stop multiple times to ask for directions, and in doing so I noticed a police car occupied by a team of patrol persons. The female officer in the passenger's seat winked at me seductively, as if to say 'follow us'. I did not follow the police car. The next pedestrian I encountered, whom I politely asked for directions from, lifted the 'Cambridge burden' off my shoulders by providing clear navigation. He adjusted the tone of my request by stating authoritatively that I wished to get to Cambridge rail station.

I tried to metaphorically explain the epiphany to my female relative. She was not following the importance of the thread or simply did not understand. I am sure that upon her return to her home she must have advised my friends and relatives that all was not well with me.

We went to restaurants and partied at local bars. We would mainly dine in French restaurants and I would habitually order bread when feeling the weight of London on my shoulders. The French waitress would invariably lift the burden by repeating, 'Bread,' with her heavy southern French accent. I believed that the suffocating UK matrix could only be relieved by French resistance. This would account for my multiple trips to France. These were to release the built-up pressure of London life. Acceptance of the bread offering was linked to the relief of stress.

Meeting up with my female relative at the Notting Hill carnival and continuing our time together was also fun. Whilst enjoying the West London festivities, we did get separated. I was determined to make my way home with no map nor any need for instructions. I was not sure which path to take. Cans of beer were illuminating my journey, and whether by luck or design I managed to arrive at a pre-designated tube and rode it all the way home. The beverage journey vindicated my power!

During my relative's stay, I even caught up with one of her male friends who had studied with the nephew of the former king of Greece.

I walked my relative to Angel tube station and she told me to stay safe. I said I was fine and that she should keep safe and I questioned whether or not she would be OK. The positioning of the Greek king and Cambridge, whilst not being entirely magical, were resolving in my mind into me touching celebrity greatness and embarking on a spectacular journey. Little was I to know that I was actually psychotic and there was nothing real about either my thoughts or the colourful experiences they were augmenting in my altered state of mind.

Watching television was exceptionally painful as I could feel all transmission cryptically referring to me. Live television was particularly tough. I had to adjust my seating position as it was uncomfortable watching your life transmitted in high definition.

I recall one night seeing an advertisement on television for airline flights to Israel. I should note at this stage all radio and television I consumed was, I believed, communicating with me. I called El Al Airlines and asked for a seven-day return trip to Tel Aviv. They asked me why I wanted seven days. I replied that I thought that would be all I would need to take in the sights. The airline and I could only schedule four days to accommodate seat allocation.

I arrived at Heathrow with my flight booking code and proceeded to the El Al Airlines check-in counter. At this stage my estranged wife wished to return to our Islington apartment and, not wanting to see her, I had to leave the apartment in a hurry. In so doing, I popped into the local laundrette and did some quick cleaning. There was some detergent left over. I kept it in my backpack en route to Heathrow.

Travelling alone to Israel aroused suspicion at Tel Aviv customs. In the obligatory customs information sheet I listed my residence abroad as simply *Greece*. They singled me out and took me into an interrogation room. The security team were very friendly and questioned why I had laundry detergent with me. I explained that it had been left over from London and I did not wish to waste it. They asked me where I was going to stay in Tel Aviv and I said I would enquire at the tourist information desk. They did not seem concerned and allowed me passage into Tel Aviv. I knew that they would be following me during my whole journey. At the information desk I was directed to what was described as a 'good hotel'.

I walked for miles and miles in the middle of the night in those Tel Aviv streets. I took tours into Jerusalem and the people were exceptionally nice to me. I passed through all of the sacred sites and wore a yamaka near the Wailing Wall where rabbis were reading prayers.

During the Jerusalem tour the guide asked me my background and I answered that I was Greek. He simply replied, 'Neighbours.' He was a *good* man and, as I was travelling alone, we walked and talked in close proximity during the entire tour. Traversing the paved Jerusalem streets he pointed out where Jesus Christ's hand had allegedly left an indentation on the side of one of the stone walls. He asked me to place my hand on it. Sure enough it was a perfect fit. It was true that at the time I felt like a modern-day saviour. Not sure why, but he also advised me that the Romans had killed Jesus Christ.

Despite being totally out there, I never once, even in my altered state, compared myself to Him. In hindsight my devout religious upbringing was one of the last remnants of my profile that I could truly claim had remained more or less intact, during my many highs and lows. In fact, without faith, I am not sure where I might have ended up during my journey.

At the conclusion of the tour and for reasons unknown to me, the guide advised me to follow my nose. I interpreted this as smell being the only remaining sense that I could call my own. His comment made me evaluate my existence and admit to myself that I was being swept away by supernatural forces and that my own senses were no longer under my guise. I was not afraid, though. I embraced it. After all, life is a journey, not a destination. You cannot plan your whole life. It should be embraced for what it is: engaging, brutal and always challenging. It is not a mathematical puzzle in which you spend time trying to achieve a desired result. This is the beauty and savagery of life. You are faced with so many options that ultimately your multiple rises, plateaus and falls are based on decision-making. Take away your manual decision-making process and throw yourself to the bosom of the crowd and you will be truly free!

In my confused state of mind I was drawn to the power of Israel and felt safe and comfortable there. I managed a trip to Masada, where I was telepathically communicating with the female tour guide. There were also British tourists on my trip making sure that I was guarded and safe. They would never leave me alone. That was my complex para-doxical belief at the time: the love-hate relationship. I adored Britain and its people and at the same time they infuriated me because they were always exact and meticu-lous in detail. This also included the multiple telepathic conversations they were having with me. It felt as though they were marginally more retentive than me and this of course annoyed me to no end. I wished to roam free but their planned existence and formulaic pursuit of life conflicted with my free-spirited approach.

This bidirectional telepathic communication asked questions of my past and commanded me to destroy items I had acquired during my life. I would contact establish-ments I had loyalty card programs with and have them ceased. This was completed one at a time following careful schizophrenic direction. I had to confess all bad deeds I had committed during my life and provide reasons for my actions and reactions. I just about came through unscathed and would find cryptic substantiation and acceptance the next day on some inner-city London magazine stand. Now what would happen?

I was spending incredible amounts of money, but all along knew this would be returned to me via corporate intervention. Even though I had long resigned, I could hear voices in my head urging me to take my estranged employer on a journey which included Israel. I slept well whilst in Israel and felt very much at home there. At the time, I wished to reside there permanently. I considered the nation of Israel to be the global arbitrator in my 'good versus bad' conflict. It was, after all, in my mind, *clean* and clear!

In fact, many months or even years later, I would borrow a book with instruction on the Hebrew language. I was determined to reside there and had to, of course, immerse myself in the culture and language. I believed that the connection I had made in Israel had accelerated my spiritual transcendence. I had propelled myself into elevated spirituality which touched all souls and spirits before me. I was indeed a god! As I could not concentrate for long periods of time, the book was inevitably returned pretty much the same day.

Returning from Israel I found my wife and her visiting sister in our apartment. I still had a key. We barely spoke whilst I picked up some personal belongings.

I caught the next flight to Athens. I arrived at my uncle's place and explained that my wife and I were experiencing a difficult time. I did not wish to burden them with my troubles. I stayed there for a while.

In their Athenian suburb there was an Internet café and I used it to communicate with prospective employers. I was still unemployed at this stage and finding it more and more difficult to find employment.

The application forms I submitted must have been confusing, especially the email I sent to Bloomberg. I asked for two secretaries, one with a warm Californian accent and one with a cool Britannia accent. I also asked for a regular supply of male moisturiser, remembering my painting tradesman and the fact that I wished to stay young and glowing forever. There was a series of phone calls to the Bloomberg UK reception which, although friendly, did not assist me in achieving employee status. I did see one advertisement from Bloomberg requiring a Greek-speaking correspondent. I submitted an application stating that I spoke the Greek language. In my mind I believed that Bloomberg were trying to reach out to me without making it seem like assistance. We could not make a connection.

At this time I also applied to American organisations as I was increasingly becoming attracted to the freedom of the USA. I recall a conversation with controlling British voices in my head, where I said that I would rather be pumping petrol in America for minimum wage than be a highly paid corporate slave in the UK. I would verbalise, much later, this sensation to my mother, stating that Britain was Great but there was nothing like America!

My obsession with American freedom really came to the fore whilst working in London. I was suffocating in my current role and wished to transfer to our USA office. I had to find out visa requirements. I used another employee's phone to make the call to the USA embassy, so that they could not trace the call to my extension. I was totally paranoid at this stage. As is the case with most American embassies you needed to leave a message via the voice prompts. I did not leave a message. I left the office and headed towards the USA embassy in London. Emblazoned on the building were the words *In God We Trust*. The words seemed to stand out amongst all of the surrounding crowded buildings. I headed into the building and approached the front desk. The security guard said I should enter into the Green Card lottery to obtain an American visa. It was the only way. I was reluctant to heed his advice. I would make it to the USA and freedom – one way or another!

Ten

Trying to obtain employment in the UK, once you have voluntarily resigned, is quite difficult, as I was finding out. The same recurring question would be asked: 'Why did you leave your previous employment?' It was hard to explain, so I would try to deflect the question by stating that the management team were not in cohesion and that we all just had different and conflicting ideas on the way the company should operate.

I was set on a UK banking career but nobody would progress my application. I tried HSBC Midland, NatWest and Barclays. I did not try Lloyds; I believed this organisation to be sacred as it would underwrite many other organisations. I even tried Credit Suisse. I remember my Credit Suisse preliminary interview. I stated quite forthrightly that I was a 'Greek national' and did not need to complete a résumé.

I would call the main phone number for these organisations and ask if there was any message for me. Invariably, there would be an immediate article in the media (radio, television or print) with some subtle reference back to me included from these companies.

I remember being particularly aggressive towards the recruitment arm of NatWest. The next day there was a television interview with a NatWest employee stating the reality of hard economics. This was of course an implied response to my harsh tone. Yet, even as I watched the interview, I felt as though NatWest were protecting me from the outside world. I was becoming a harboured individual and this pleased me immensely.

Aligning myself with various UK recruitment agencies was also quite fun. One such organisation agreed to meet me at their London office. My mind at this stage was racing and when I got there they said that I was lucky and they had an offer for me. They escorted me to meeting room seven. However, somehow I felt it all a bit of a staged set-up and wanted no part of this 'lucky intervention'. I threw the interview and was candid and almost insulting in my responses. It felt like a theatrical production. It did not feel real. It was as if it had been rehearsed just for me and upon becoming aware of the whole situation I could not take part in the plot enactment. You need to understand that I constantly craved accidental occurrences to generate progress, or, if you like, magic!

So I headed to a secretarial firm to redo my curriculum vitae. The only lady in the office was beautiful and assisted me with the construction of my CV. I would make multiple visits to her Islington office for assistance with the required information inputs. But, again, it felt like a performance was being put on. There was a gap between real time and perceived time. It was frustrating me to no end. Every time I headed over there she would have her purse and handbag ready to head off with me on some exciting journey. The voices in my head, however, were racing and advising me that this was all fake and it was not happening sponta-neously. I was aware in my mind that she was ready to leave with me but because of the circumstances we could not just leave together. There was no natural occurrence creating the magic. I put this down to British bureaucracy, which did not want to have any surprises but preferred everything planned out. No shocks, please; we're British!

I even contemplated changing industry career paths, via some historic, pre-ordained, superimposed process. Whilst employed at my pre-London marital home I had had an epiphany. This had translated to the creation of a flowchart documenting the various stages of the marketing of a product. Even to a spaced-out marketer it would have seemed quite bizarre. It plotted the course of early adoption to laggard adoption and, of course, product institutionalisation. It used obscure references to existing corresponding popular products and service offerings. There were diagonal lines drawn all over it linking them in some quasi-mathematical consonant resolution. I kept it with me for reasons known only to myself and took it with me to London.

During my employment hiatus and wanting to industry-hop, I contacted the managing director of a media buying agency. How did I pick that particular one? As I was browsing a newsstand, the voices in my head directed me to pick up a magazine and purchase it. As I read the associated articles, it was as if the agency were summoning me to contact them and 'close the gap' in their theme of recurring media buying patterns. I would continue to purchase the weekly magazine and felt empowered because the articles, according to my mind, were summoning me to the industry.

I mustered the courage to contact the managing director via telephone. The first time he was unavailable. The second time he was busy. The third time I got through to him directly and informed him that I was impressed with his comments in the magazine and looked forward to working with him very soon. He asked me to flick over a curriculum vitae. I did and included my spaced-out flowchart, outlining that it was 'not indicative of all thought processes'.

Whilst I could not claim media as mine due to the fickle nature of the industry, I felt as though I had made a 'clean' connection without a manufactured interjection. I was also conscious of leaving media buying the breathing space required to allow for creativity without my universal stifling. Media buying would be left alone, as would advertising!

Later on I would read an article in the same publication about thought processes. Those bastards were plagiarising my words, so I ceased buying the magazine.

By this stage I was convinced that Greece should become a superpower. This theory was compounded by the fact that during a stay in Greece I heard the television state in a scratchy schizophrenic tone, 'The government wants answers.' I interpreted this message as a warning because I had risen far too high and I was becoming aware of secrets I should not be aware of.

The 'Greek' voices in my head also ordered me to obtain a French passport. This too was compounded by television-transmitted instruction to obtain a French passport. It occurred during a Greek news broadcast and the delivery of the message rose above the tone of normal transmission. I knew the passport request was directed to me. The commanding tone was slightly distorted and yet still succinct. But how to obtain the French document?

I flew off to Paris again. This time I was enraged and felt that after all I had done, customs were not permitted to check my status. I entered Paris and nobody checked my passport. I am not sure to this day how this was even possible. I was free-flowing thought into the Parisian air. My mind swirled and danced carelessly out and over the River Seine. Paris was mine! I did not wish to close off France because this would have resulted in stifled thought congestion. I had become French. In my mind I had obtained a French passport. It was sweeter than any piece of paper or documentation and that was all that mattered. I was floating on an air of invincibility.

My manic behaviour was also becoming uncontrollably erratic. I recall being penned up in a London hotel room full of pure unadulterated rage. I called the Greek priest of a local London Orthodox parish to try and express my strange feelings. He asked me to visit the church so that we could speak in private and in person.

After the telephone conversation, I felt a power consume me. His thoughts were seeping from beyond the telephone line and invading my mind. Much like in a science fiction thriller, his presence was infiltrating me. I had to react quickly! I picked up an empty glass and hurled it against the wall. It smashed into hundreds of pieces across the hotel room. I repeated the act and then, satisfied that I had broken the curse, fell asleep.

My nap was interrupted by two members of the hotel staff who promptly knocked on my door. There was a middle-aged lady accompanied by a young man. I could tell that she knew that I was totally out of control, but I had a wickedly defiant look in my eye. Come on, the British won't give up on me. It's not like them to.

'You're welcome to stay here for as long as you like ... but you are going to have to pay for the glasses.'

With that I knew that they would have my back for life. I had gone through every high and low known to mankind and yet they would still support me. British Steel!

I arrived back in London after my Paris visit and dared not return to my apartment, as my wife was residing there now. I headed off to another expensive London hotel, where I based myself. My unlimited credit card was taking a hammering, but I was free.

I would spend countless hours pacing all over London, marking my territory by telepathically corresponding with the unknown and uninvited voices in my head.

I recall visiting the Bank of England, but they would not allow me to proceed inside their offices. This was virtually the first time anyone had halted me on my journey. I returned that night saddened by having been stopped. This was very unlike the British characteristic of voyage with abandonment into the unknown. I had got to know the culture quite well and, despite the rigidness of the British, they shared the same passion for journey and adventure that I had. This was the true British spirit. Set foot on any soil!

On one manic excursion around the streets of Islington I was carving up the footpath with my footsteps in an attempt to extend my range of audience captivity. This included wilful or resisting participants. I was gathering momentum until I came across the entrance of a local pub. For some reason it felt eerie and uncomfortable. A rather large Anglo-Saxon exited the establishment and in a very frightening tone stated, 'Now then!' He had been deliberately placed there as a human stumbling point to halt my meandering passage. I did not look at him directly and simply ignored him and turned back. From my peripheral vision, however, I could make out the façade of his torso and that he had a very solid and tall frame. I returned to my apartment and wrote a poem, which I believe from memory was entitled 'Ode to Savagery'. I would release my toxicity in verse. An unstamped envelope made its way to some literary headquarters with the contents of my poem. Thou shalt not silence me!

That same day or maybe even that night – I was starting to lose track of time – I wrote a short story titled 'The Pilot'. It was about three pilots who were challenged with the task of flying as close as possible to a bridge which was just jutting out above sea level. The first pilot set a national record by flying in close proximity to the bridge. When asked how he would like to be rewarded for his achievement, he stated that he wanted shares in a pay television licence. He was granted his wish. The second pilot was American and he smashed the previous mark set. When asked for his reward, he stated, 'I do not wish to pay income taxes for the rest of my life.' His wish was granted.

The third pilot was Greek and he hopped into his plane and actually flew under the bridge. He left the scene and was never to be seen again. His wish was granted. Anonymous glory!

The point I was trying to make in the story was that different nationalities and different people value different releases. Not everyone is fixated on material prosperity. This is the beauty of life. The more you transact, the more you learn about yourself. Even in my darkest moments, I never lost sight of the emotions that bind us as a race. We all celebrate life differently and learn about it further during our personal journeys. The pursuit of material possessions and publicised recognition will not grant you full inner peace. Master thyself and thou wilt master life's meaning!

Then, in the early hours of that night, or the next morning, I penned 'The Earthling': the misguided adventures of a friend of mine who, without a soul, was trying to stake his place in the world. Whilst I cannot recall the whole story, it ended with his future-dated death, at age thirty-nine. He could not pin down his place in life. The conclusion to be taken from the story was that you need to unify with others and understand that you are not alone in the world. As human beings we need to connect with others. We need to resolve our conflicts and understand that we do not stand alone. Sanctity in isolation is flawed, because ultimately you are referencing your own touch points and not enhancing your existence. Socialistic? Maybe! In any event, another envelope, another trip to the UK post office. That's right: 'No stamp, please; I am insane!'

I returned to Athens, where I stayed for forty days or so. It was a relaxing time and I enjoyed it thoroughly. We even spent a week at my uncle's seaside house just outside the

Athenian jungle. The beach house was cosy with enough rooms for all of us and I would spend the mornings walking down to the beach. There were rocks where you could sit and watch the sea tide come in. With each gentle undulating breaking wave I would try to reconcile thought and clear my mind. It was proving very difficult to do so, but the sea air was having a mellowing effect on the rage which had built up inside me.

The week was up and we returned to the concrete of the city.

It was during one of those incredibly hot Athenian nights that I was gently awoken by what I thought was a firmly placed hand on my abdomen. I had felt it during my sleep. In my dreamlike state I clearly heard a female schizophrenic voice recounting a haunting passage. It came to life in crisp tone. It was from my poetic creation, all those years ago. No one could have possibly known of its existence.

. . . I cannot despise but I can learn to dislike an image of me
That deals out these cruel blows and still insists belief in Thee . . .

Eleven

From Athens I planned my entry into the USA. At the time I was having what I believed was thought communication with Michael Bloomberg, who I was convinced had confirmed my appointment in Bloomberg's New York office. I booked the next flight to New York City to start my new life in America. The land of freedom.

Early on that week I had called the New York office of Bloomberg and had asked to be transferred to the HR manager who had elegantly and eloquently responded to my initial emailed application with, 'You're joking, right?' I had immediately responded with a detailed email assault on her misgivings about my importance.

The receptionist who answered my call was steadfast and transferred me unconditionally to my required destination. As she transferred the call, I could physically feel the call being relayed and visualised the endless miles of cable caressing it through its journey. The best way to describe it is as like mercury travelling though glass, efficiently slithering down the pipe. There were multiple transfers and each time I was greeted I was unconditionally transferred. This was true power. I had forced my presence down the telephone line and every vocal greeting knew who I was.

I hit the destination's voicemail and it felt like a brick wall. I analysed the HR manager's profile as one of the pillars of the system that would invariably kill off my uninhibited gliding. The theme of global human demarcation points of presence would continue to obsess my thoughts. It was my challenge to circumvent them or defy them. She was one of them. Much like the Polperro service station attendant.

I met an Irish lady on the plane to New York City, whom I believed British Airways had placed there deliberately to satisfy my now intense physical urges. We chatted and flirted and agreed to hook up once we arrived in New York. I am not sure why but I advised her that I had been with a lot of women. She replied that she had been with a lot of men. She moved closer to me so that our bodies were touching. The arm rest had been raised and if we could have we would have had sex then and there. Wow, how great was this?

The Irish lady asked me about my background and I informed her I was Greek. I then began telling her about the true spirit of Greece as recounted in the Greek national anthem. She asked me to whisper it into her ear. At the time it felt like a national betrayal and I had to ward off commands of non-compliance from the nationalists in my head. I did recite it and then kissed her softly. I felt the Hellenic burden somewhat lifted from my shoulders.

She passed through USA customs easily as she was meeting her sister in the Big Apple. I, however, was halted at customs and produced both my passports. The customs officer took my non-Greek passport and stated that I would not be needing this one. I presented my Greek passport. He told me not to lose 'this one'.

Over the intercom, the announcer stated, 'Welcome to the States.' I warmly smiled. I knew the announcement was meant for me. The customs officer asked me why I was smiling. I made up some excuse. He proceeded to ask me questions with simultaneous instruction that I did not need to answer any of his queries. He was anal-retentive in carrying out his tasks and was annoying me. I concluded that he was a damn Yankee. The adjacent officer, however, was smooth and cool and I baptised him in my mind as all-American.

I advised the Yankee that a representative from

Bloomberg was meeting me at the airport. I could mentally feel their presence just beyond the border. There was, of course, no one there! He called the Bloomberg office and they did not know who I was. I had no USA visa and when the customs officials asked how I was going to live in New York City, I replied, '. . . with my credit card . . .'

I spent what seemed like five hours in a detention area. I was also photographed and fingerprinted. International vagrancy?

I was getting bored and during a break in concentration from the customs officials, I did step three or so metres beyond the demarcation line. That's right: I had for all intents and purposes crossed into the United States of America. I smiled to myself sheepishly, feeling my journey was not a total waste of time.

After much deliberation, the British Airways team agreed to fly me back to London free of charge. Got to love Great Britain! At this stage, I believed that the UK would catch my fall unconditionally during my journey. We had struck up a deal. I remember saying to one of the British Airways officials, 'I am in your hands, yeah?'

She turned to the customs officer and said, 'Return him to London.'

He – the USA customs officer – then turned to me, looked me directly in the eye and stated in no uncertain tone, 'You will be back!'

I was thereafter led away by four rather large airport security officers and on to the next BA flight to the UK. They asked me what the issue was. I replied, 'Corporate complications.' They just smiled.

I would not be halted and thought carefully about a circumventing solution to the dilemma. The USA would not tolerate two vagrant entry attempts, so I had to think it through. Upon my eventual return to my parents' home I borrowed a book about the Native Americans and their history. I tried reading it to find hidden clues which would link me to the Cherokee or Sioux tribe. This was in order to re-enter the USA as a native without the need for a traditional passport. If I could somehow find a common thread it would assist me in gaining American passage. I even located a local travel agency dealing exclusively in USA travel. I made contact with the American owner and planned an itinerary. I bumped the scheduled meeting and gave up on the idea as it was all getting too hard. That would have been some customs conversation to try and explain.

I came very close to returning to the USA but thought that it might spoil the magic of the country I had created in my mind. It also became more apparent to me that our worlds should not collide as we were somewhat connected through the mysticism of my journey.

During the flight back I was not accompanied by any pretty woman and the stewards and stewardesses were not their usual accommodating selves. Were they getting tired of me? Did I favour America over Britain?

I screeched back into Heathrow and checked into another expensive London hotel and started feeling the warmth of the city again. My reasons for hotel choices ranged from subtle hallucinatory commands to direct orders. I had initially rejected what the city was about and now felt as though it was my spiritual home.

During one of these multiple stays at expensive London hotels I was again exceptionally hypomanic. I was totally convinced that the CIA were following me and that a group of American guests had been sent to my adjacency for my own protection. The voices kept on telling me to either break politically right or break politically left. I ventured out into the streets, turning left and right according to formal instruction from the friendly voices in my head. I returned to the hotel and asked them to bring my luggage down from the room so I could leave the country. I had to get away. I was suffocating. Literally!

This particular hotel was close to Heathrow and had a shuttle every thirty minutes to the airport. I approached the concierge and asked for a ticket for the shuttle. He asked for two pounds. This was the prepaid shuttle fare even for guests. I had no money. I had just spent my last cash on a pair of black designer Calvin Klein jeans acquired at the local town as a trance version of the James Bond theme played in the store. In fact, I had caught a cab to the nearest town centre to purchase the jeans and refused to pay for the cab ride back. I recall advising the taxi driver to invoice the UK nation and slamming the door on the way back to the hotel. So here I was, no money and no ATM nearby, breathing with difficulty, and this bureaucratic clerk was asking me for two lousy pounds. I turned to a hotel guest standing next to me and asked for the fare. He was American and had heard the conversation. He was happy to assist someone down on their luck. Like magic he appeared to help me. I knew the USA would always catch my fall irrespective of the circumstances.

I arrived at Heathrow full of rage and called a relative from the airline carrier desk phone. They bankrolled my one-way ticket from Heathrow back to my parents' home. I specifically asked them not to take out insurance on the flight. I was superhuman so I did not need cover. I even recall arguing with the booking agent that I did not require any insurance because the UK was mine and the Queen knew who I was and she would protect me and all of *my* people.

In fact in the hotel I had been staying at, earlier on in the day, I was wandering around the administration section when I stumbled upon an unoccupied office. There was a desk with a computer on it. On the computer screen there were only two words in very large print: *EDWARD WINDSOR*. To my surprise the computer was unlocked. I deleted *EDWARD* and entered my first name. I then went back to the hotel reception and asked if there was any mail for me. I was expecting a British passport, as the voices had me convinced that this hotel was a passport exchange centre. There was no mail. The magic did not continue that morning. I asked again for any mail. Again, there was none. In my mind, I could not specifically verbalise my requests because it would destroy the plot and this was all part of the game which I was being lured into. During the whole time I always felt I was complying with both my destiny and 'official' duty. I was a soldier executing a telepathic plan with surgical precision. Everything had to be perfect in an abstract colliding sort of way!

It was a long day and I recall having telepathic communication with the President of the United States, our company's chief executive officer and our company's chairman. I was reaching out to all of them to continue their individual journeys and allow me to continue mine. I would carry the torch for all humanity. Why not? I had broad shoulders and could carry the world's pain. I could sense the trio's longing to experience my freedom, via subtle replies in the form of television, radio and print media. In fact I had met the CEO and chairman at various official work functions. Upon meeting them I had felt my profile rising considerably to the point of mentally over-powering them. I could not contain the power within me. Like all of my other similar experiences it was eerie at first, until I learnt to adapt and manage the power.

Another day and another hypomanic state. I do not remember where I was but I do recall the ferocity of the command in my head. The vocal tone resembled a distorted audio recording and before I knew it I was heading toward a gymnasium in Hampstead. I was convinced that I needed to make an identity switch with a Greek secret service agent. On the way there a couple of Greek-looking ladies passed me by on the Upper Street pavement, heading in the opposite direction. I felt the warmth of one of the girls' hands as it brushed mine accidentally. I was being protected by my own people, but not openly. I was being secured by the magic and coincidence I was creating.

The journey to the gymnasium was like a slow-motion dream. It was not happening in real time. The best way to explain it is that it was like a sensation of elevated spirit when the backdrop is applied just for your main starring role.

I arrived at the Hampstead gymnasium in a pool of sweat and I grabbed the vacant locker key at the same time as the person I thought was a secret service agent. Our eyes met and locked and we knew that we could not make the exchange at that particular point in time. I let it go and headed back to my Islington flat. A connection could not be made.

This would be a recurring theme. There was always a gap between what I was thinking and what was being acted out. When it all synchronised it was artful and beautiful. Everything had brilliant colour and definition and the audible tones were clearer and sharper than anything previously known to me.

The majority of the time, however, try as I might I could not connect normally with anyone or anything. There was always what appeared to be this gap in timing. It is very difficult to explain to normal people but it was like a dream where you are falling endlessly into the ether and you are awoken just as you are about to hit the ground. During my psychotic tenure I would never awake but, rather, would carry on in this non-connecting dreamlike state, endlessly. It was incredibly frustrating and I could not sense closure nearby. When I became aware of the nature of the conversation thread, it would render that silo useless, so I would move on to the next one expecting different results, which would never materialise. The experience was of course blanketed by insanity. The reason I could not establish a connection was because I had completely lost my mind.

In fact the same day that I visited the gymnasium, I was lying down on the couch in my Islington flat when I clearly heard a bird singing as if it were communicating with me. The bird's voice and my thoughts would be released into the air like a call-and-answer song. My thoughts escaped my mind and ventured unadulterated into the homes of many, and I heard a female neighbour of mine move a chair each time my brain waves slipped into the global subconscious. Every time I leaked a thought, she would move a chair. This would cease the filtering of thought and the cycle went on for hours. The television was switched off and there was no music playing. She was protecting me. I got on well with her and she would invite me for tea on a few occasions. She was a good friend. We would chat in passing, as she resided in the apartment directly above mine. A local guardian angel, if you will.

Dejected from the missed gymnasium exchange, I travelled to Knightsbridge and sat down at a café. A South American waiter took my order and I asked for a Coca-Cola. He blurted out, 'One Coke,' and returned with the order. I could not say 'Coke', because my wife had told everyone during a London work function – accidentally, of course – that I had taken cocaine when I was younger. I knew that would stop me becoming a company director and I had to wear the embarrassment and shame. The waiter had read my mind and, in one defiant act against

British stubbornness and stiffness, stated 'Coke' in no uncertain tone. This was a nice moment. He had lifted the burden from my altogether misplaced mind. South America was behind me! Viva la revolución!

I did not end up drinking the whole Coke and as it had been served to me in a can I took it with me for the tube ride home to Islington. Somewhere on the Northern Line I found myself in a carriage which was almost empty except for one guy who was sporting military trousers, a black jacket, a bizarrely printed T-shirt and, of course, a Mohawk haircut. Whilst I was not afraid, I was not in the mood for confrontation and tried to motion him telepathically away from me. He did not heed my warning and sat in close proximity to me. I held tight to the can of Coke as I believed the representation of the American iconic brand would protect me from this now apparent threat. I looked straight ahead clutching that sweet can of Coke and left the journey as the train carriage arrived and emptied the potential threat at Angel tube station. During my weakest times I would always resort to American institutions and organisations for protection. I believed that they were protecting me globally. God bless America!

In a mad rush I was summoned by forces to head toward the Pimlico library. I ventured there in a state of total rage. I would either dedicate my day to a museum trip or enrage the locals by visiting the library and unearthing the tortured Greco-Anglo history.

As if by design, I arrived at the library with no need for directions and headed straight to the history section. I grabbed a short paperback on the history of modern Greece and flicked to the relevant section on the Greek Civil War and Britain's involvement. I got to the page very quickly and even in my confused state it felt a little mystical. The history burned deep with me at the time. Not that I am, or ever was, a communist, but, in my mind, Britain's involvement needed to be addressed. Many people died and many Greeks were persecuted at the hands of the British. I would also make a historic statement. All in my insane state.

The male librarian glanced at me in disapproval, as if to say, 'Why not go to the museum? Why did you have to bring this up now? We are looking after you! You are virtually a local now!'

So, back to the hotel where I was staying I went. I turned on the television and systematically, telepathically crashed the sterling against all of the major currencies. It was like magic. What I was thinking was being executed on the financial markets. My thoughts were being replicated on bourses all over the world. The non-British financial markets were with me! The sterling would bounce back later that afternoon, but for that moment I was controlling finance. My will could translate rage into monetary degradation.

My lovely Audemars Piguet watch had stopped working, so I headed off to an Islington watch repairer. The man behind the counter was very friendly and we struck up a conversation. He stated, 'It's a good watch.' This was interpreted in my mind as meaning that my Swiss-French friend was good. I welled up with tears. I left the watch there to be repaired in a week. I never returned to pick it up and consequently never saw it again.

I would immortalise my Swiss-French friend in a poem I wrote whilst living in London, titled 'Chance Meeting in the Northern Hemisphere'. I put this poem in the UK post for my Swiss-French friend with no stamp and no address. It was simply sent with her first name on the envelope. By this stage I was convinced that, being a superpower, I did not require any postage. *They* were going through my mail, so they would find its destination. I can only recall a few passages:

> *He did look upon her. She did will him to … Where art thou, fair maiden?*

At this point I was making a distinction between good and bad. Whilst this is an arbitrary condensed observation of the world, it guided me in my mental categorisation of people and the specific action I would take thereafter. I believed that I was solely responsible for preserving the forces of good against the forces of controlling evil. The best way to explain this is in the following detailed series of events.

Whilst we were still married and both employed, I was listening to music in one room of our Islington apartment. My wife was watching television in the other room. She headed off to sleep and I found myself alone in the lounge room. The soundtrack CD for *The Crow* had been left opened on the coffee table. I thought that this was a sign from my wife, who I believed was good and was protecting me through my journey. I picked up the CD and on the back was a series of numeric digits. Thinking they were a secret code for a telephone number, I punched out the numbers on the nearby cordless telephone. A lady answered. I do not recall where she was or even which country she was in, but I hung up. As I hung up the phone a chill ran down my spine and I felt as though some massive evil force was going to take me up to heaven or some morbid variation of it. I wasn't scared. I was terrified. I called out to my wife to ask what the hell was going on. She replied, 'Were you born in a tent?' In my mind I had positioned this apocalypse as associated with controlling forces taking me to some sort of twisted version of paradise or hell and I was resisting. I am still not sure what my wife meant with her comment, but just hearing her voice calmed me down. They would not take me away tonight.

I was checking in and out of London hotels and European countries, including Austria, rapidly. At this point I believed my thoughts were being read by most of the known world and that I was bordering on conscious control of others' subconscious thought and emotion. During a visit to Vienna I attended a recital which included a performance of Mozart's 'Eine kleine Nachtmusik'. I felt that as I shifted my thought processes, the ensemble were moving with me and I was creating variations in their tempo. I was effectively controlling their minds. This was scary and I was a little uncomfortable with so much power. In time I would learn to control it and embrace it.

There was a similar occurrence when my wife and I attended a performance of *Jesus Christ Superstar* by Andrew Lloyd Webber in London's West End, when we had first arrived in London. We had great seats and I could manage eye contact with the performers as they cast a gaze into the crowd. Every time I changed position in my seat, however, the tempo would slightly alter. It was a strange feeling and yet very empowering. The orchestra seemed like miniature puppets within my control. I felt like a giant which could manipulate the whole group. I particularly enjoyed the guitarist's playing and granted him licence to improvise. He carved it up fluidly and articulated my thoughts on the fretboard – note for note. Man, he was really getting into a groove and so was I. The actor portraying Jesus Christ was not connecting with me, however, and it felt as though he was alienating me from the audience. He was not English, but rather an international guest performer. I interpreted his non-compliance with my thought movements as an insult and commented to my wife later that I felt he had over-performed the role in lacking the necessary delicacy and finesse. It was an odd night but I reconciled my power as a natural progression of my snowballing grandiose personality profile.

I would walk the London streets, circling Buckingham Palace to protect the royal family, which I had resisted claiming as my own. I left multiple gated exits so the royals could venture out and about.

I would also contact Greek Orthodox priests and arrange to meet with them and try to explain my rising behaviour. However, each time we met it felt like I was stronger than the Church itself. It was hard to explain, but even during religious mass I could not contain myself and my thoughts. It was as though my mind was leaving my brain and floating into the air. Communion could only contain me and calm me down for a matter of minutes.

My mind could no longer be closed and anyone with the right power could read my mind. So what did I do? I used it to pass my message across to billions of people and I would receive responses in my mind or even as clear audible voices in my head. It was scary and yet fun and engaging. I was controlling the known world and I was on a crusade. Yet at the same time I felt trapped like a slave in a vicious cycle of manipulation by controlling forces. They were using my powers to get their messages across. It angered me and I could feel the rage in me increase each time. I longed to be free to catapult into the ether, unabashed and unashamed.

My thoughts, however, were scrambled, ambiguous and delightfully insane. For instance, I believed that the abstract accidental collision of ideas and events was the true representation of art and the pure way forward. If events and thought processes were deliberately controlled, the progress achieved could not be pure. I had by no means read up on any theory related to this doctrine, but was nevertheless convinced of its truth.

*

Shortly after my spectacular departure from my employer, I was heading home to my Islington flat and had an eerie sensation of awaiting registered mail in my letterbox. It was my severance statement and confirmation of employment release. I picked up the letter and headed towards the front door. It was very close to twelve noon Greenwich time. As I was sitting opening the letter the phone rang; I did not answer it and instead allowed the machine to answer the incoming call. It was exactly twelve noon. The defiant automated American voice on the answering machine *swallowed* the frail British-accented caller trying to leave a message. America had my back!

Countless application letters followed to American organisations. They did not immediately reject my submissions. They were just curious why I had chosen their companies. There were never any spelling mistakes either back or forth in the *communication* with these companies.

I would head back to the small secretarial office in Knightsbridge where a fluent, charming, middle-aged British woman had co-authored my résumés on professional paper. It was very near the café which had so eloquently served me Coke previously. The middle-aged British woman would ask me how I had found her as she was in an obscure location and mainly worked on corporate accounts. The truth is that going through the local directory her advertisement was more pronounced than others. It literally jumped out in front of me. I did not dream of telling her. It was what you could best describe as a print media hallucination. These hallucinations would continue randomly for many years.

On the taxi ride back, the experienced London cabbie approached the intersecting street adjacent to my flat. I advised him to turn right. He said he could not because there was no right turn into that street. I advised him that I lived there and that I knew my neighbourhood. I would turn right there regularly. He remained firm and not wanting to debate the point, as I wanted to get home, I asked him what the fare was. We both looked at the meter at the same time. It was £20.20! There was a pause. I opened my wallet. There was exactly £20.20 in it. Upon entering the apartment, I called the Islington council, who confirmed that there was in fact a 'no right turn' policy for that street. They thanked me for my call and let me be. London Pride!

Twelve

I was running out of money and contemplating returning home to my parents' house. I did not wish to leave London; however, with no job comes no income and London does not come cheap. So I decided to return to my parents' home temporarily.

As I was departing Heathrow, the announcer stated what I thought was, 'He is leaving London with a tear in his eye.' It was true. I had welled up. No matter how frustrating the city was to me, it was home and I had learned to love every aspect of London life.

On the flight back home, I believed that BA had arranged for a beautiful Spanish woman to sit next to me. There was a vacant seat between us and we started chatting. I was overtly friendly and she was very engaging with a beautiful Catalan accent. I convinced her to place her head on my lap and softly caressed her face and the side of her body. She was intoxicatingly attractive. I would kiss her cheek every so often and she enjoyed it. I did not sleep but allowed her the freedom of my lap and she lay there peacefully. When the plane landed, we embraced and kissed passionately and exchanged email addresses before departing on our separate ways. I would never see her again, nor would I have any contact with her.

Another interconnecting airport, another beautiful woman. She was Dutch. I worked it out from her accent. She was having her image transcribed onto a canvas with a black sketching marker. A crowd made up of mainly men had gathered to watch the portrait come to life. She had a firm and yet inviting gaze. The crowd, including myself, were spellbound. The Dutch woman was dressed appropriately but not expensively. Provincial if anything, but she was pure beauty with high cheekbones and strong facial features. At the conclusion of the painting the commissioning artist asked for money. She did not have any. At least seven men planted the required cash on the nearby table. She smiled and walked away.

I somehow ended up back in London and went straight to my favourite Islington library. I spent that afternoon researching the events surrounding Dunkirk during World War II. I deliberately skimmed the factual events so that they would not cloud the beauty of the Netherlands. I decided at that point that the nation was a close ally. The national Dutch airline would comfort me on some of my frequent European benders thereafter. Dutch courage!

I am still convinced to this day that British Airways were setting me up with beautiful, available women. This is because this happened on multiple occasions. I was their star representative and they were my airline. I was protecting their flights and they were heeding my hedonistic telepathic requests. I was convinced of this telepathic communication, so much so that on one occasion I deliberately did not pick up my suitcase from baggage claim as I knew they would find me. They contacted my parents' home after rummaging through some paperwork I must have left behind and politely instructed me to pick up my case from the local airport.

This constant thought of 'controlling forces' monitoring my every movement was deeply entrenched in my mind. In fact, I believed that my prescription glasses had a micro-camera that would relay messages and conversations to some sort of global control room. I would mess with *their* minds by taking my glasses off periodically, just to disjoint their focus. After all, it was all just one big game and I was at the centre of it. I even went so far as to literally flush my work mobile SIM down the toilet.

The story goes something like this.

Whilst working in London, I had left the office one day in a state of sheer paranoia. I was telepathically conversing with one of my English colleagues about us running Britain and controlling a puppet Prime Minister and puppet Chancellor. I believed that secret agents were following me, so I walked briskly and entered a hotel. Inside the hotel bathroom, I took off my glasses, dismantled my mobile phone and flushed the SIM card down the toilet. I washed my hands and put my glasses back on. In my mind I had to telepathically justify to the world why I had taken off my glasses to flush the SIM card. I settled on hygiene. I was in the toilet, so hygiene took precedence in my actions. Prior to disposing of the SIM I was in a state of total paranoia and could feel forces overwhelming me mentally and physically. This act restored some peace to my fragile mind.

When asked by HR why I needed a replacement SIM card, I told them the truth. I stated that I was being chased by secret agents and had to dispose of the SIM card in a safe place. They replied with a laugh and a smile.

The hotel had been singled out because it was near a musical centre of interest. Musicians were global ferries protecting me from the secret service. Musical landmarks would protrude against the backdrop of buildings, guiding the way to the 'safe house'. I was not alone in my quest and journey. The perpetrators of justice were akin to my vision of global unification.

Mum and Dad were glad to have me home. They obviously knew that my wife and I had separated and I began to chill at their home. All the while, however, I was growing restless and my mood swings were out of control. I also had a heightened sexual appetite which could only be satisfied with multiple visits to brothels. In fact in the space of four hours in one manic episode I had encounters with five prostitutes, including two at a time twice. This went on for a long time and of course it was very expensive.

I actually got hooked on one French-German prostitute who had a European underground rock scene look about her. She would entertain me regularly and the sex was aggressive with vampiric biting. I could also tell that she was enjoying it to no end as she would let me extend my session for free on many occasions. We were getting close and quite chatty. Our last session was amazing and intense. I kissed her on the cheek and stated, 'Liberté, égalité, fraternité.' She kissed me back on both cheeks, smiled and winked. That would be the last time I would ever see her. Just the way I liked it and, as I had written in 'Death by Politics', 'alone and regrettably sane'.

Some of the brothel sessions were quite hilarious too. Prostitutes would ask me what I did for a living. I would normally respond that I shuffled countries and that I was involved in the finance industry and travelled the world extensively. They were impressed. The sex was wild and exhilarating. I could not get enough and I found the brothel the only place I could find peace.

One night, I was chatting to one prostitute who told me that she was trying to make it in the music industry. I advised her that I knew everyone in the music industry. I found it amusing that she kept harping on about not being able to get a big break and all the while I was telling her that I was connected in the music industry. She could not have known that I was insane, and yet she did not even ask for my assistance. Wow, that night was so funny! We had sex four times in the space of one and a half hours. She told me that was the first time she had done it that many times with one guy during one session.

The divorce settlement occurred around this time and it was very unkind to me financially. I lost a lot in terms of money, property, chattels and monetary opportunity. In fact, had I continued in my career progression and not become ill, I would have been a very wealthy man today. I am currently not wealthy. As I believed opposing lawyers were listening in on my conversations and thoughts, I did not respond to any written communication. This resulted in a monetary strip-down during settlement. Going by my memory, I may have even settled many of my affairs from some European location. That would explain the hefty legal costs including telephone air time. Got to love the legal fraternity. Justice embracing hope? More like justice embracing justice.

During my stay with my parents I tried to recreate the fluidity, articulacy and creativity of my earlier poetry. I could find neither rhythm nor inspiration. My vain efforts resulted in obscure results such as one poem titled 'Ostrich Eggs'. They were all burnt at my hands so that no one could trace them back to me. The same reason I used to burn my original poetry. If I was going on an unadulterated journey, I needed to rid myself of all addictions and footprints. There was one, however, untitled, which was just two lines and I was proud of it:

> She beckoned the correction of a digital cross,
> It left a small scar and she was helplessly lost ...

Around this time I had struck up emailed communication with a lady and these lines would be my signature sign-off. She only knew me as Byron; as a tribute to all of my flirtations and lovers alike I would travel to Sounio, Greece, and pay homage to the inscription of romantic poet Lord Byron. She loved me! The poem was about a woman finding religion again in the modern world and having to give up something for it, to be true to it. This release of some personality profile would inevitably have future impact, hence the small scar.

I spoke of a similar theme to my wife during our Islington days. It was the natural progression of human-kind contained within the backdrop of musical periods: Medieval, Renaissance, Baroque, Classical, Romantic, Nationalistic. In order to make the transition from Romantic to Nationalistic you needed to give up something. In Beethoven's case, his hearing. Once you nationalised, your thoughts and life's work were recorded as part of your country's national dossier. The next step was to be the highest point of your country's national profile or well and truly break free on your own identity. If you broke free you were a socialist and if you remained within your country's profile you were right-wing.

When I met my Swiss-French friend in Geneva I handed her a book on classical handwriting as a gift in thanks for showing me the sights of her city. She quickly and girlishly blushed momentarily. I asked her to stay classical. She knew that I would protect her and the Protestants for life: the same protection I had shown her when she had visited my wife and me for dinner in Islington on one occasion. At the restaurant, I helped her take her coat off and placed mine on top of hers. She understood the imagery. She was, of course, European!

I tried contacting my Swiss-French friend multiple times and in so doing started aggravating her. Each time she would ask me not to call her again, but, alas, it was like a drug. I needed to hear her voice. She ended up installing an answering machine. I left countless messages but to no avail. I would always play the same phrase from the same song recording across the telephone line.

On one occasion, I wanted to organise a dinner date with her. I had an overwhelming feeling that she was near my parents' home. I was guided to the local telephone directory by some superhuman force and instinctively flicked it open. I am not sure how, but it opened on the page of a Swiss-French restaurant. I knew I did not need to book a reservation. We were now far from requiring normal methods of communication to transact. That night I suited up and drove to the Swiss-French restaurant. There was no booking in her name. I drove back disappointed. She had stood me up!

The next day, having remembered my childhood sweetheart's parents' telephone number, I decided to give the residence a call. I tried many times but no one answered the call. I would hang up after seven rings as I believed that was enough time to have a reply. In my mind, if the system stalking me was going to go backwards then so would I. I had amassed a substantial amount of distance in my global pursuits and if it was amounting to nothing then I too would regress. My childhood sweetheart and I had shared many steamy and passionate nights as teenagers and I could always sense her smell around me. During hypomania the sense of smell is heightened and I would always *feel* her aroma around me, even when in foreign countries. It was feminine, distinct and clearly identifiable. During our younger years we were very much in love and could not bear to be separated. I longed for her again. Her parents would know her whereabouts. If my Swiss-French love would reject me than I wanted my historic first love of the heart. But, alas, the phone rang off into the ether, destined for some incomplete resurrected love story. What to do next?

I purchased a personal computer to hook up to the Internet. It was not brand new and had some bugs. Nevertheless it allowed me to re-enter the World Wide Web and cast an online presence. I met a married American woman in a chat room and convinced her to provide me with her number so that I could call her. Our chats were incredibly sexual, filled with dirty talk, and when I called her I felt that I had reconnected with the USA. She asked me to visit her so that we could meet face-to-face. I even recall planning the whole trip, but her marital status created a moral dilemma. So I did not fly to the USA. Instead I sold my computer to a group of friendly bikers, who thanked me for the opportunity to purchase *my* personal computer, and I then cancelled my Internet connection.

That brief encounter was exciting, however, and I will never forget her voice and our communication. I also believed that communicating with her would allow me access to the USA portal and that everyone in America was listening in on our conversation. So I played up for the audience! I advised her that everyone in America was my friend and that I would soon join them all in the land of the free and home of the brave.

Back at my parents' home I was also gambling excessively at the local casino. Yes, I was counting cards on the blackjack table. Somehow, I had clarity in my mind when gambling and could count cards clearly and methodically, or alternatively I was just lucky, as I was consistently winning. Whatever the formula was, I was always ending up on top for some reason. I reasoned in my mind that I was indestructible and that this talent was due to my higher elevation of spirit, mind, body and soul. I would inevitably develop a gambling habit later in life, though. But the rush! Oh, the rush! Pure adrenaline!

The winnings would invariably find their way into the bra compartment of a twenty-something lady escort. You've got to love 'after hours' fiscal management.

Driving restlessly for countless hours in my father's car was the only way I could clear my mind at the end of a hectic day's 'work'. I would get as close as possible to vehicles on either side of me to induce a rush of invincibility. I crashed the car multiple times and it was only by chance, or divine intervention, that I did not injure myself.

On one occasion I reversed straight into the path of an oncoming vehicle careering into the passenger's door. The lady driver who emerged from the vehicle was visibly shaken but thankfully not injured. We exchanged details and I asked her if she was OK. She smiled and replied that she was fine, so I smiled back at her. She must have known who I was and how important I was, which is why she did not make too much of a fuss over the accident. I started flirting with her as I found her very attractive. The circumstances and danger associated with our meeting seemed to arouse me and I yearned for her.

That night I would visit a brothel and embark on a sadomasochistic adventure that would last for hours. As if by premeditation and foresight I would realise my daytime fantasies in the confines of a parlour of Eros during regular nightly sessions.

The vehicle access ceased, however, as my parents would only allow me to use the car for necessary trips. This was because I had inflicted infinite and expensive vehicle damage and degradation. Taxis would be the preferred method of transportation and, of course, they would suck up much of my remaining savings.

During those long drives I would try and work out political and national secrets. In my mind, as I was destined for greatness, I needed to align myself with a political power. But which one? Being fairly central, or even neutral, with my points of view, I decided to align myself with all parties. I would send cryptic messages telepathically or via letters with no stamps affixed. For example, I would mentally communicate with the American Republican Party headquarters indicating that being right-wing did not mean you could not roll out a strategy of socialism. Of course, I would also communicate with the Democrats and advise them that being left-wing did not prevent you from encouraging a financially prosperous enabling policy. I wished to connect with all life forms and all minds. I had a ravenous appetite but constantly felt that I could not be contained within normal parameters assigned to thought and reason.

Desperate to locate, in my mind, national secrets, I would think through all the points from which nations could draw their strength. I even believed that right-wing Americans would think of Fort Knox when trying to remain strong-willed. However, becoming aware of this secret would render it useless in my mind, because I had uncovered it. The cycle would repeat until I had exhausted all possible thought-resolving combinations and I decided that I needed to unite the world with my thought analytics. This was only a temporary solution, as I believed that placing thoughts into people's minds was unethical and contravened the global pact which the powers of 'good' had agreed on. Good people could only read minds, but dared not place thoughts. So I resolved this with an essay I wrote and telepathically communicated to Oxford University, indicating that I was 'bordering on conscious control of subconscious emotion and thought'. That is to say, I could not be held responsible for thought which escaped my mind and found its way into other people's brains. The escaped thought could be triggered by emotive or subjective reasoning, reacting to an abstract collision or accidental series of events. I had argued my point logically and objectively and felt that I had safely averted a moral dilemma.

In fact, during my stay in London, as I was sitting down finishing breakfast at an Upper Street Islington café, I recall a group sitting down to order at the table next to mine. I am sure I overheard a middle-aged man say, in a confused tone, 'Bordering on conscious control of subconscious emotion.' To this day I am not sure whether he actually said it or I only thought I could hear him say it. In any event, his quizzical look focussed on me and I looked away. I paid the bill, which had simultaneously arrived, and went on my way. I was defiant in a non-engaging, disarming manner. My thoughts were inadvertently reaching the global audience. However scrambled they were, they were being delivered to multiple mental touch points.

Travelling the Underground, I also recall a moment where my thoughts escaped involuntarily. A beautiful woman entered the carriage where there were multiple vacant seats. Somehow my thoughts accidentally leaked from my mind and entered her brain. I was inadvertently asking her to sit next to me immediately. As if drawn by some magnetic force she complied and sat next to me despite the vacant real estate. I was scared at this time because I had not deliberately willed her to. Some super force had dragged her to the adjoining seat. I felt responsible and guilty at the time and did not quite get over it for a long while. Could it be that I was superhuman? Could it be that if my craft was mastered I could change the course of history? I had a conversation with the forces and logically extricated my position as a purely accidental leakage of thought.

So I checked into a local London pub to have an alcoholic beverage and relax my increasingly manic state. I overheard the bartender stating, 'I wonder what the papers will say tomorrow.' I presumed he was Greek and was pleading my case in a non-confronting manner. Sure enough, the next day there was an article linking my thoughts and behaviour in a cryptic analogy. For all intents and purposes only those 'in the know' could decipher the code and meaning of the article. I would be summoned to that newspaper because it was illuminated boldly within the confines of the newsstand. It reached out to me invitingly as if written specifically with reference to the day's proceedings. It was life imitating and mimicking life and I was totally wired and felt totally alive.

Newspapers, radio and television would document my journey and I would soak up all of the media and playfully and methodically interact. By discarding material after it had been read in carefully, methodically placed rubbish bins across Greater London, I would partake in the puzzle, each location and reason why known only to myself. I was helped and guided by external forces controlling me and directing me to each location.

These same forces would also inhibit my routine behaviour, daily and regularly. I would systematically turn left and right and obey or disobey traffic signals depending on the voices' mood for that particular time of day. There was no subjective or objective denominator or resolution. Simply put, it was a series of random events that would resolve naturally in some sort of weird consonance. This went on for a very long time and as you can imagine it was very frustrating.

I would even write an essay on objectivity and subjectivity entitled 'The Objective and Subjective Duck'. In hindsight, it did not make any sense. It tried to convey how the two personality traits differed and how the objective duck would try to defend their position logically, whereas the subjective duck would emotively argue their position. I addressed it to the University of Leeds – that's right, no stamp. Why the University of Leeds? A colleague of mine (from my work in London) had graduated from there and I was resolving her over-the-top subjectivity in the essay. I was, after all, objective and defiantly logical.

I clashed with my Leeds friend but she had a soft spot for me. The woman in question was full-figured but nevertheless very attractive. We were good friends and I had sensed she was protecting me from afar when I had travelled to Israel. She had a Jewish background and an ancient Hebrew surname. I had linked her to Israel and I had confided to her that I would be travelling to Israel very soon. It was as if she had passed on her blessing to me for an inspired journey. I had tried to explain to her that I had accelerated knowledge prowess and that I could soak up six years' worth of knowledge in six days. She had sort of seemed impressed. It was important for me to have her respect and buy in. I believe that I did, as I recall telepathically communicating with her during my employment hiatus.

One day in the office it was overcast outside and I asked her to join me for a coffee. She did not wish to walk the short distance to the nearby cafeteria because it was gloomy outside. I summoned all of my internal and external strength to change the weather. It was remarkable! The sun popped out from the clouds. She turned to me and said, 'Mister,' in a resolute tone. I could change the weather and she acknowledged that I had also acquired the power of a woman, which is of course greater than any man's power.

This was not the only time I believed that I had transformed weather conditions. Post-London, and whilst residing at my parents' home, I was feeling total annihilating rage against the world. At the exact time that I released my mental frustration, the sun hid behind some clouds and the sunny summer day turned into a black haze. I commented to my parents that a black curse on the weather had occurred. Shortly afterwards a neighbour passed away. I resolved this mental release as being the cosmic forces balancing the universe. My built-up rage had caused a death. This time I was scared. The outside air was thick and smelt of decay. The sun did not appear again that day. It was the height of summer.

My female friend from Leeds kept asking, 'Why you?' as if to say, 'Why are we all following you? What is so special about you?' We became good friends and even shared a train ride after a company exhibition we were staging in

Brighton. It was our organisation's push to promote our brand in the marketplace and a team of us were manning the stand. A very attractive woman from a nearby stand stopped and chatted with me. I was elated by her presence. I was also married at the time. I followed her to her stand and in so doing felt every fibre in my body alive and tingling. It was not like first love or even wilful lust. It was pure elation and animalistic. It was like my skin was peeling off my body and I was enraged with pure fire. I am sure my body temperature must have exceeded its normal acceptable levels. She was gorgeous but I was married. In hindsight, the availability of many women and the importance of my global journey added to my eventual decision to end our marriage. Notwithstanding this, at the height of our marriage dissolution I was a free-wheeling, free-thinking psycho sociopath. I could hardly connect with anyone anymore and my Brighton babe would be just another passing encounter.

At the end of the exhibition and during the shared train ride back to London I started chatting with my Leeds friend. I must have confused her to no end with my ramblings on behaviour and my importance in the world. She either pretended not to listen intently or dismissed my cryptic speech as arrogance, confidence or just boyish extravagance and boasting.

I would communicate telepathically with her for almost a year after my resignation. I did so because I felt that she understood me. By the same twisted logic I had utilised to classify personalities and people, she was basically good. Just a little boisterous and dogmatic, but good.

Whilst residing at my parents' place after my return from London, I would also check out expensive apartments to rent so that I could be alone with my thoughts and govern the known universe. The interaction with the various real estate agents must have been bizarre from their perspective when I tried to explain my line of work. I was, after all, soon to be a very, very rich man. I even started buying an expensive wardrobe of clothing and household goods in preparation for my repatriation. On one shopping spree I insisted on the most expensive towels in the department store. There was nothing significant about the articles of purchase. They just happened to be the first items I had viewed upon entering the department store. I was pleased to receive the bathroom products after paying a handsome price for them. I decided to cab it home and was picked up by a man I thought was an ex-Russian KGB agent. We chatted very briefly, as superpowers do, before he dropped me off at my parents' house. He was new in town so asked me where to from here. I advised him to stay right. What I metaphorically meant was to stay politically to the right. He understood. Russia was subtly on board!

I also recall going for long walks along trekking paths and overhearing the conversations of fellow walkers and joggers. One time, I heard some walkers stating that 'he' needed to destroy the photographs of his past. I would inevitably return home and destroy any photographs which were non-compliant. By 'non-compliant' I mean any photos with cigarettes and alcohol references contained within them. I was cleansing my history and as I would soon become an overlord I needed to rid myself of any controversial reference points. I even went so far as to flush chopped-up film down the literal and metaphoric toilet. It was cathartic and released me from my shackled past. With every swirl I felt another layer peel off the weight plastered onto my shoulders.

Thirteen

During one intense hypomanic rage I could not take it any longer. I was literally battling with the voices and forces in my head. I had returned late from a club and was possessed by a maddening agitation. Upon entering the house and in one final act of desperation I declared my parents' home 'Greek soil' in defiant riposte to those controlling entities. As I began tumbling into the void, I sensed the whole house turning Greco-British simultaneously. I could feel the presence of ancient warriors from Greece and historic figures from Britain. It was like nothing else I had experienced before. They were occupying the same space and time. Whilst chillingly eerie, it was reassuring and, again, paid homage to my power and all-consuming presence. I could make out the murmurs of thousands of years of history and I managed to sleep peacefully that night. I had effectively zoned my parents' home so that I could feel the warmth of Greece even when I was far away. The British attended the party to keep the faith ablaze and alive. As I entered the zone the sensation would be Greek. The air would literally have a Hellenic smell about it. As I left the zone, the air would taste foreign. A primal ambassadorial residence? Was I creating a historic footprint in the present? Would I be the anointed leader? Would I lose my anonymity? What would my destiny be?

Frequenting the local Greek embassy, I would also feel enveloped in Greek nationalism. With each visit I would try to resolve national secrets, each time trying to find some clues giving insight into the country's history of greatness and global dominance. We were a rising force and in my mind I was our leader. Subtle instruction and communication reinforced my beliefs, but I had to keep all acquired secrets sacred and never relinquish the key. I had made a pact with the government, or so I thought, to protect the nation from having its treasures revealed and to take the acquired knowledge to my grave.

For some reason, whilst I worked in the UK, some of my British colleagues would quiz me on the secrets of Greece. I would, of course, not oblige. This would frustrate them to no end. They would eventually give up in their pursuit. I would feel vindicated!

One English colleague did push the issue, however. We both possessed leadership qualities and had mutual respect for each other's status, but it did not stop us trading national mental blows. A group of us decided to play a five-a-side match one afternoon at a nearby basketball court, after leaving work earlier than usual. As the office was multicultural it was of course England versus the rest of the world in an international football friendly. We edged out the competition narrowly and I do remember mentally willing the football to hit the post on the last English attack.

Relaxing at a pub, after the game and after we had showered at the nearby facilities, my colleague asked me again directly about the national secrets of Greece. He seemed to believe that my power had been granted to me nationally as part of some Hellenic doctrine. He retired his glance and in a matter-of-fact tone said, 'Your family secrets.' This indicated that the secrets I was harbouring were family-based and not national.

That night I lay awake in thought analysing and deconstructing what he had said. I was formulating a family behavioural equation and nearly resolved it. I was interrupted by the friendly tone of the ringing telephone. It was my mother, stating what I heard as, 'Now you know our family secrets.' Could it be that our family's secrets were Greece's secrets? I lay further awake analysing the facts. It was true. We had reached equilibrium with the Greek government. Our behaviour was national and as a Hellene that was as far as I could go. If I pursued differing personality traits, I would be rising over and above my country's national profile.

During my highs and lows I always believed that someday my amassed knowledge and power would be handed over to the Greek government. They would retire me in a comfortable apartment with a Greek wife and I would fall into anonymity.

Again, I could hear the murmurs of ancient warriors in my head. This time they seemed obliging, helpful and willing to show me the way. It somewhat completed my cycle of defiance and created a mental plateau for my journey thus far. I was reincarnated as the orthodox warrior.

Another miserable morning and another fit of rage. I contacted a financier and transferred all of my personal financial resources into one Swiss financial institution. I believed that only there would my finances be truly safe. This was partly because of my Swiss-French friend and partly because of the paradox I had created in my mind. This paradox was a love-hate relationship with Switzerland. In fact, I poetically explained my position in an anonymous letter addressed to the country of Switzerland with, of course, no stamp. I do not recall the specific destination of the letter. Does it really matter? It would have made interesting reading at the Dead Letter Office.

As I remember it, my Switzerland-bound letter had a word which was not contained within the Oxford English Dictionary. It drove me crazy. How could I have made such a lexical error? It was a rushed oversight. I, of course, wrote another letter to the Oxford University Press pleading with them to add my word in their next edition of the dictionary, due to a number of nonsensical reasons. I do not believe that I was successful. Again, no stamp!

This was not the end of it. I caught a cab to the local Swiss embassy to personally hand over all of my private financial documents. I made it to their level via an elevator; however, their offices were closed. I interpreted this as a superpower stand-off and returned to my parents' home and hid all of my financial documents in the attic, including all of the receipts from my overseas escapades. I would later burn them and many photographs to extinguish my past in an effort to rewrite the future.

Off to the British consulate I headed. Why? I had a severe toothache from around my London time and wanted to know if the consulate could recommend any *good* dentists.

I had previously visited a dentist in London after enquiring via telephone. The receptionist at the UK dentistry had advised me that the visit would be free. I reconciled this as part of my compensation for services rendered to the British government in keeping the peace. The dentist joked about his receptionist allowing me a free consultation. I knew that he was just covering up for what would soon be a government-funded existence. I did require some root canals which I would later have done near my parents' home, all the while knowing that any expense incurred would be reimbursed.

The British consulate were curious why they would recommend a dentist. For, you see, during my sanity hiatus I believed that the world was a mass of literal and metaphoric minefields. I had to interpret cryptic messages and clues from all reliable sources to navigate my path and reach my eventual resting destination. A destination which would resolve the demons plaguing my existence daily. The demons that would wake me up in the middle of the night because I was directed toward Angel tube station to stop a crime being committed. An attack on humanity could be thwarted if I could arrive at the destination, instructed by the voices in my head, just in time. The voices would literally carry me over to the anticipated scene of the crime. This occurred regularly and was haunting in its solitary communication. I would of course be the only one who could hear the voices and I felt obliged to use my superhuman powers to avert a disaster.

The local dentist I eventually settled on, after much research, was of Balkan descent. During every one of our multiple appointments I would ask her if I was required to pay for every visit. She stated of course I was. I would reply by stating that I would require a receipt. This went on regularly and habitually. It must have frustrated her. The receipts would be methodically filed in chronological appointment order and the X-rays maintained.

The root canals were painful. The intrusion was required, however. I knew that I had to preserve a perfect appearance as I would soon be heralded a hero and all monies would be refunded and my future existence would be monumental. I was overwhelmed by vanity and wanted to be above all in perfect representation to the expectant global fanbase. Perfection in my body and spirit would starve the demon scourge and would allow me freedom from the cycle. This was always my deepest wish. To be released from the infinite ongoing madness within.

The demons would not stop there, though. They would come to me in vivid nightmares beckoning me to global destinations. Forcing me to obey instruction or suffer the consequences. I remember dreaming about a shootout scene between police and threatening passengers at Heathrow airport. The next day I arrived at Heathrow and I believed that the scene was being enacted exactly as I had dreamt it. Policemen to my left and policemen to my right illuminated the terminal. The exact same passengers were criss-crossing the floor. The warmth of an embracing hand I had dreamt of did not come forth, though. I told myself that by arriving at the airport I had stopped a horrific crime just with my presence. I waited for someone to hold my hand and take me away. There was no reassuring hand and no warmth. The place was as cold as always. I would return despondent and yet vindicated for letting the world turn with me for another night.

I recall tearing up many photographs and burning many articles of designer clothing. This was to cleanse my existence. The ritual of tearing up photographs was to induce an apocalyptic reconciliation of my journey thus far. I had to rid of myself of all that reminded me of the past so that I would be free to glide into the future. Fortunately enough some photos remained intact as I could not locate them. Each time I destroyed a photo I could feel another layer of burden released from my soul. It was cathartic, in a twisted, demented sort of way! The designer clothing was burnt because I was conscious of the label rising up on me. It felt as though the label was taking over my thought processes, and when I became aware of it I had to destroy it and not wear it again. The likes of Versace, Armani, Calvin Klein, Dolce & Gabbana and Bulgari were reduced to a desert of ashes. But I was free!

Around this time I developed a medical condition where the last two fingers on my left hand were completely numb for a number of days. I had them tested by a medical practitioner and was told that I required overnight surgery to decompress an ulnar nerve in and around my elbow. He provided me with a list of locally based surgeons and asked me to select one. As I had no health insurance I would have to pay for the whole procedure.

The list of surgeons supplied to me caused a dilemma in my mind. Which one should I select? I carefully analysed their surnames in my mind and tried to reconcile the profile of each one based on the history of their surname. Two names stood out from the list. In fact the two printed entries on the supplied list seemed bolder and brighter than the other names. It was like the list was communicating with me. I settled on one after much deliberation, but kept the second one as a back-up in case I was not completely at ease with the first selection.

So off to the surgeon's office I travelled, at a predetermined appointment time. The receptionist was British and had a very non-confrontational style but did not warm to me. I assumed that the British people had placed her here to protect me from any harm. The atmosphere was cold but I felt safe.

She called out my name and I entered the surgeon's office. I immediately requested that all microphones and spy cameras be turned off. I also asked the surgeon if he was in any way connected to the CIA. He warmly smiled and said that he was not. I am still not sure why he did not find my behaviour odd at the time, nor why he did not summon the relevant authorities. In any event he explained the procedure and I asked him how many times he had performed the surgery. He said countless as it was a routine procedure. I was at ease. I believed that his personality was genuine and good.

I felt safe and relaxed during the pre-operation stay in the hospital room. The nurses were friendly and I was regularly flirting with them. They played along.

The decompression procedure went well; however, I woke up in a strange state of mind. I was again feeling paranoid and I was not sure what had happened whilst I was under anaesthesia. My gown was messed up and I felt my underwear riding up my body as though it had been misaligned due to manual adjustment or intervention.

They released me from hospital and I was picked up by

my parents and cooled my heels temporarily during the drive home. When I arrived at home I was convinced that something else had occurred during the routine surgery. I did not like the anaesthetist and felt as though a female member of the surgical team had been eyeing me in a strange way. But what could have happened during the operation? I came to the conclusion that they had somehow taken a sperm sample from me and were already initiating a plan to create a super-race from my non-compliant donation. Enraged, I personally delivered threatening letters to the whole medical team. I had obtained their practice addresses from the multiple invoices I had received. I was cryptic but also direct in my letters, saying that if anything other than the decompression of the ulnar nerve had occurred during surgery they would feel the full force of my wrath. I was obsessed with the idea that, having attained perfection, I was now under the watchful eye of science to assist with the advancement of the human race.

So I wrote a letter to the second-choice surgeon from the original list asking him if my post-surgery exercises were fine to continue with. I sent him the stick-figure illustrations of the various exercises. He actually replied to me in writing stating that I was well on the way to full recovery and that the prescribed programme was what was needed to regain full strength in my left arm. I checked out his surname. It was a Hebrew surname and he had been placed in my journey for my protection.

Fourteen

My behaviour was beyond bizarre by this stage. I was actually taking instruction from the radio and could understand the subtle placement of cryptic messages, occasionally erupting into laughter for no reason or crying myself to sleep at night based on minor associations of these cryptic messages with my life thus far.

As you can tell I was getting increasingly frustrated and increasingly paranoid. Again, I was going on long drives in my father's car and listening to music searching for hidden meanings. On one such long drive I was pulled over by the police for a routine car inspection. The policeman opened the bonnet and took a look inside. I had an overwhelming urge to shut it on him because I thought he was evil, but for whatever reason, thankfully, I resisted. This same policeman would later take me from my parents' home into the local psychiatric ward. Let's call it what is: a mental asylum!

I would leave the family home and fly off to the UK on multiple occasions and continue my random European journey. I would return unenlightened and increasingly in a despairing state. On one of my last trips I had invited suspicion from family and friends who must have alerted some authorities. A specialised local team including many armed policemen came to my parents' home to ask me questions about my frequent, spontaneous overseas trips to London. They asked me if I believed that I was communicating with the television. They were not psychiatrists but nurses sent out on an evaluation call. I answered their questions with bizarre responses. From my answers they must have assessed my mental state.

The next night there was a knock on the door. Two

122

female ogres as hideous as Hades himself stated emphatically, 'Schizophrenia!' They were joined by the policeman who had pulled me over previously and his partner. My mother burst into tears and as I was leaving I said in Greek, 'Stay with the British!'

The cops took me from my parents' home in the back seat of the police vehicle and buckled me up with the safety harness, like a common criminal. I was then driven to and admitted into the mental health unit of a local government hospital.

Nothing would be the same again. My whole world collapsed at that very moment. Even during my most psychotic scenes this seemed neither of this world nor fabricated. It was demonic and disabling. I knew then that there was something horribly wrong. Not necessarily with my mental state, as I could not have understood my illness whilst being insane. It was like being abruptly awoken and not knowing whether you were still having a nightmare or it was playing out in real life and real time!

Upon entering the psychiatric ward I was petrified and visibly shaking. A local nurse tried to calm me down and I kept on repeating that I had been betrayed by my family. I was trembling and had no idea of what was going on. I would be assessed by a psychiatrist in the morning and they led me to my room, which would be locked down for the night. Welcome to the void. Return your mind to sender. It isn't coming back. Neither are you!

That night was one of the worst I have ever spent in my entire life. All the lights were switched off and the darkness in the room spread to my heart and soul. I was lifeless and it felt like damnation. There was a lady occupying a room adjacent to mine. She was screaming as if possessed by a demon and must have been banging her head against the wall. Every wooden thump was like a knife through my racing pulse. My heart was accelerating and in my isolation

I felt like a vulnerable victim of circumstance. Her episode lasted all night. Although I could not see her, her screams were terrifying. In my schizophrenic state I mentally closed off my room mathematically to stop any evil from entering. I reconciled the longitude and latitude of the room and fenced myself in. I did not sleep at all that night.

The next morning I was attended to by a government psychiatrist of Chinese origin. He was trying to advise me to stop my confused thoughts and settle down. My mother had also told the Chinese psychiatrist that I had once picked up a knife, believing there was somebody outside the door trying to get in late one night, whilst living with my parents. I refused to speak to him because I thought he was an idiot and I asked them to get me another psychiatrist. They ordered me another psychiatrist who was of Russian background. I asked them to replace him as he too was aggravating me.

The next day they assigned me a British psychiatrist. I was much happier. He was thin, with glasses and short blond hair, and spoke softly. I felt more at ease with him. I believed that the British people had sent him to plot my escape back to London. He prescribed medication and advised me that I was schizophrenic. I disagreed politely and was non-compliant with the medication. They would administer it and I would go back to my room and spit it out.

During this time I also asked to be seen by a priest; I believed that he would be able to assist in getting me released, because the *system* had contravened my ecclesiastical upbringing and beliefs. He arrived and to my surprise was from the same region of Greece as my mother. With confused thought I shared a cigarette with him, and tried to explain to him the horrific first night I had spent with the head-banging patient. I told him of how I had sealed my room and asked him if this was by holy instruction or not.

He looked at me strangely and advised me that I should comply with the medication, as everyone takes medication and it is OK to do so. I asked him if it was possible to have the medication blessed. He did not seem to think it was necessary. He said I would be fine in three days or so and that when I got out I should visit him so we could discuss spiritual themes. Upon my release, I would visit him and we would discuss these themes, as he tried to explain that I had fallen off the edge slightly and that it would not be long before I was back on track. How little did he know at the time that I had fallen completely off the rails and no church, by design or not, was going to help me.

I told the hospital psychiatrists what they wanted to hear and somehow after a week or so they released me into my parents' care. The government team would visit my parents' home regularly to check up on me, and, fearing another stay in the hospital, I must have fooled them with regard to medication compliance. With the hindsight of sanity, this was probably the first time I had severe doubts about the validity of government agencies and their thoroughness.

During various stints at my parents' home I was feeling totally out of control. There was a flood of weird behaviour reflecting my thought processes of the time. I would send letters to various organisations from different postboxes. The letters would be cryptic by nature and controlled by communication I was receiving via print, radio and television. With respect to newspaper articles, I believed that they were directly addressing me in some sort of secret code. I remember reading a small obscure article about Sylvia Plath's life and death. I reconciled this as direct communication based on the fact that she was by far my favourite poet. This constant reconciliation of action controlled by media was overtaking my thought and obsessing my subsequent actions. It was like magic. I would be thinking something and the media would validate my thoughts.

Back in my time in London, I had brushed past someone I thought was a very famous American lawyer. I had then sent a letter to a Japanese bank requesting protection for the music of John Lennon and having it administered by this famous lawyer. These random acts would manifest into pure obsession and literally spin me off the planet. I even remember having telepathic conversations with celebrities. They were clear, succinct and bi-directional in nature.

Routine activities were also proving to be very difficult to complete. I would eat food and spit out what I thought were the mind-altering substances. I would stand up when it was OK to do so and sit down when controlling entities allowed me to do so. Radio on, radio off. Television on, television off. Now, which article to read in the local newspaper? The page would virtually turn itself to the relevant highlighted section. I could sense the telephone ring seconds before it would actually ring and it would send my heart racing. I was being controlled and it was very dangerous.

From my recollection I actually sent a letter to the media-buying managing director in London outlining how I was to be paid on my forthcoming employment with his organisation. I even melted wax and sealed it with the key of a discarded family passenger vehicle. The key was also sent in a separate letter to a neighbouring destination. In my warped logic, he could identify me from the key's identity and match it with the seal of the envelope. Not only was I insane, but I had carved out my own reason and logic which I assumed that engaging presences could understand.

The letter also calculated my ridiculously high and incredibly bizarre salary demands. I factored one American cent for every member of the population of the country which I had conquered. This amounted to a handsome annual sum. There was also a multiplying accelerator for further national acquisitions determined by the impact of my presence on those geographic locations. I reasoned that my intrinsic value could be calculated mathematically and I even provided details of a legal firm which could attest to and validate my total contract value. The terms and conditions would of course be sent and administered telepathically.

The most ferocious example of my schizophrenia was having a dream where I heard a very clear name being read out to me by someone with a crisp American accent. During this dream I also witnessed the enactment of a mass murder. The next morning I was convinced that the news feed I was watching, with respect to a recent shooting spree in the USA, was about the person I had dreamt of the night before. I did not flinch as I watched the story unfold. The identity of the killer was the same as the name read out to me in my dream, the night before. It had not been a normal dream. I knew this because during normal dreaming the images, voices and scenes are not as clear. The voices and images in my dream had been in high definition. At the time I believed it to be the only way in which the government of the USA could grant me access to their national secrets. They had let me in.

I pondered the revelation for a while. Did the US government actually have the ability to foresee criminal activity and alert their inner circle? Was I now a member of that inner circle? The greatest power on planet Earth had invited me into its private regime. Was it in fact that powerful?

I prayed that night for American soldiers fighting overseas. The next day the cable news channel ran a story on a soldier who had taken a sniper shot to his helmet. He had escaped with no injury. My prayers had been answered. More stories ran that day. In a frenzied reporting period I saw peace break out in regions around the world. My crusade was coming to fruition. I truly believed that I possessed the power to end centuries of war and violence, right from the comfort of my own home!

I would also experience positive, mystical and magical dreams and not be confined to nightmares alone. That was the trade-off. During the *good* dreams the images of people were like airbrushed celluloid reels. Famous people would appear to pay me homage. People whom I had admired were also represented in their full glory with extravagant gowns and elegant jewellery. I would awake feeling refreshed and invigorated. I knew that the endless kaleido-scope images were sent to me by angels protecting and guiding me through my travels. I would decipher and interpret the spiritual imagery the next morning and balance the ever-growing assortment of thoughts in my head.

There were some workmen near my parents' home one day repairing a pay TV cable. A severe thunderstorm from the previous night had knocked out the cable connection. They were hammering some apparatus onto a pole that day. The incessant noise went on for what appeared to be an eternity. Every hammer blow would send chills down my spine and they felt like literal gunshots. It was a hot day and I had short trousers on with no top. The sound felt like death blows and I immediately assumed they were killing me loudly. They had been sent there to interrupt my thoughts and it was infuriating me. I stepped outside and blasted them with a demonic voice and went back inside feeling aggrieved that I had let them have it. I was so paranoid that day that I could not find inner peace of any kind. I was turning into a tortured and tormented soul and

I could not find any release from the overlapping toxins which were perceived, believed or otherwise.

In hindsight, the chemical imbalance in my brain was probably creating a gap between real time and perceived time. However, we will never know for sure! In cases like the anticipated telephone call and multiple occurrences of déjà vu, it was all about the timing of the neurotransmitters from my brain.

I could not connect with other people in normal ways and there was always a gap between thought processes and actions. On the occasions when this gap was filled, it was the ultimate high. Hypomania is an abnormal high, but nothing can replicate the elation and joy one feels. It is also dangerously addictive. You want that feeling to last forever. In fact, you believe that the high is endless and that the supply can be everlasting.

I am not convinced by the theory of multiple psychotic episodes. It is one prolonged episode based on your rationalisation of your existence. It may last for decades with fluctuations in polarisation and can explode into colourful life (hypomania) or even morbid death (depression). Ultimately it is what is perceived to be real, and isn't that all you need? Think about it. What you believe to be real in any point in time is, for all intents and purposes, real. The manifestation you create becomes your accepted norm. Learn to stand and walk tall and do not overanalyse your existence!

I landed a high-paying job in a private company headed up by two Israeli-born directors. One of the directors had served in the Israeli Army, as had one of their employees. The employee was a highly trained and skilled ex-army person. I am not sure of the type of service he was trained in as he would not reveal the extent of his military engagement. We got on well, the employee and me, and would see clients together on joint visits. He was a little too sharp for the corporate world and had the look of someone who was entrusted with far too many secrets. I would later uncover that he had been involved in a crack military unit. It didn't affect me at the time but I would feel his haunting presence in my mind years later.

The directors liked me during the interview process and I leased a very nice and expensive vehicle – black, of course. I lasted two months in the job before heading overseas in a manic state to London with no luggage whatsoever.

My last day was also anything but routine. I needed to resign but could not find an *out* or a release for a dramatic exit. It was around lunchtime and I decided then and there to plot my escape. I dropped a file on the executive assistant's desk and it disabled the stacked plastic trays. This caused a minor disruption and I left, never to return. From my perspective, the accidental collision of paper and plastic ensured I had received a trigger to announce my silent resignation. I jumped into my expensive car which was parked nearby and headed back to my parents' home. A suitable track on my favourite radio station had just kicked in. I was electrified!

I then drove to a nearby travel agent and arranged my one-way ticket to London. British Airways, of course! Wanting to rid myself of all attachments that would slow me down, I gave the travel agent my PIN and he asked me what I would be doing in London. I replied, 'Finding solutions to problems!'

I arrived at the local airport with no money and no credit cards, clutching my Hellenic Republic passport. I constantly felt the presence of the Israeli employee with me. Was he protecting me or was he going to confront me in the UK?

During the flight I would only eat when the voices in my

head had cleared the food. The steward commented on the dinner choices, stating that the chicken was particularly nice. I knew his comments were directed towards me. That was all I needed. His voice seemed clear and defined. The voices agreed. The chicken was crisp and fresh, despite being airline food. I knew that the other selection had mind-altering drugs designed to keep me from reaching the dizzy heights I was destined for. The steward was looking out for me. He was risking his position and status to protect me from controlling forces.

I arrived in London at a very expensive hotel via taxi. I left the taxi and headed straight for room 10, which I believed was a metaphor for 10 Downing Street. I had stayed in the same room previously and I firmly believed that the British government was going to commission my services, when all the madness would eventually end. The door to Number 10 was locked, though.

The taxi driver followed me to the hotel asking for the cab fare. I advised him that an international transaction had just been deposited into his bank account. He was obviously not familiar with the schizophrenic economy and wanted cash. I did not have any. We agreed to reconvene at three o'clock that afternoon to settle my debt. He asked for my Greek passport as collateral, which I gave him.

I was now in the foyer of the hotel complex, which had no rooms available, with no identification, and I had deliberately left my credit card at my parents' home. I struck up a conversation with the Jamaican security guard, who was delightful. I was starving and he shared some of his croissant with me. For some reason he did not question my circumstances and allowed me to stay in the hotel foyer. There was a comfortable couch there. No sign of the Israeli employee anywhere, so I sat there for a long time.

The taxi driver returned at exactly three o'clock and we

agreed to head off to the local police department to settle our dispute. I turned to the Jamaican security guard and stated, 'Live, love, laugh,' before jumping into the cab to allow the constabulary to resolve the situation.

The lady police officer was very attractive, had a pleasant manner and was accommodating. I tried flirting with her. Despite blushing, she advised me in no uncertain terms that I had been receiving 'communication' for my actions. I denied it, but I knew exactly what she was referring to.

The taxi driver returned my passport. I agreed to transfer the money upon return to my parents' home. They smiled patronisingly, thinking that I would not follow through with my commitment. I actually transferred the exact amount. I arranged for some relatives to pay for my flight back to my parents' home, and of course I paid them back upon arrival. Even in my confused state I still somehow kept track of my debts. This must have been from studying graduate-level economics at some point in time. I would always keep receipts too, for some reason. Of course! My financial backers would want a record before they showered me with gifts. After all, I was on someone's clock, or maybe I wasn't! That was one of my many conflicting complex dilemmas. Hate, love. Right, wrong. Altruistic, hedonistic.

I caught up with the Israeli directors when I returned and they paid for lunch at a nearby upmarket restaurant. As I was feasting on my expensive meal selection, I tried to explain what had happened. Alas, in my confused state, my storytelling fell apart due to missing information. They told me that they should have brought the Israeli employee with them to expedite discussions. They also asked me why I had taken their organisation to London. I responded that it was time for them to globalise. They were neither amused nor interested and I did not like their tact or their tone. Finishing my meal, I stormed out of the restaurant, upsetting the chair that I had been sitting on. The exit was dramatic and I ended up driving towards home. I stopped at a business centre and sent the Israeli directors an email outlining how they should globalise and what the next steps would look like. They never responded and I would never see them again.

The military-trained employee did haunt my dreams for a long time to come and I felt like he was sent to challenge me on my journey. I successfully diminished his presence in my mind after a series of telepathic, logical, extricating debates regarding why he should leave me alone. He heeded my advice. I was again free to continue.

Fifteen

The day after I walked out of lunch with the Israeli directors, there was a knock on my parents' door and a different escorting evaluation team took me back to the same psychiatric ward. During the drive there, I asked them if I would be safe. They were both softly spoken young men and stated that I would be very safe. No policemen this time. Just a private passenger vehicle. They took the same route which takes you to the local airport. I assumed that they were sending me back to London. I was happy until they veered right at the intersecting junction. The evaluation team had telepathically lied. They were going to lock me up again!

I arrived at the psychiatric ward again. This time I would stay for close to a month.

I was completely insane and not taking the prescribed medication. The staff escorted me to my usual room. It had my name on the door. I was seen by my British psychiatrist in the morning. He asked me about my thought patterns and I must have confused him when I tried to explain what was going on in my mind. He diagnosed me with schizophrenia.

They were monitoring my medication intake now and would watch me until I swallowed it completely. I would of course conceal it on the underside of my tongue and dispose of it in the shower drain in the bathroom within my room. I was paranoid that they were trying to alter my mind and that the medication would be harmful to me.

A week had passed when I found myself not wishing to stay there any longer. So I plotted my escape. The entrance door was slightly ajar and I had some spare cash in my pocket. I am still not sure how the money got there.

I left the hospital via the front door and no one seemed to notice. I hailed a cab and headed straight towards my parents' home. I asked the taxi driver to stop as soon as he reached the limit of the money I had in my pocket. I would walk the rest of the one-hour-or-so journey. I arrived at my parents' home and went straight to bed. Freedom! The telephone was ringing uncontrollably. I dared not answer it.

A few hours later two armed policeman arrived and instructed me to change into clothing and accompany them. I was currently in sleepwear. One officer watched as I dressed and advised me not to wear a belt. They returned me to the hospital and placed me in the High Dependency Unit, usually reserved for violent or suicidal patients. This time my oral medication was substituted with compulsory daily dosage injections, administered by nurses and supervised by security guards. It was not pleasant at all and I was literally verbally forced into compliance, with the alternative of being *managed* by the stocky security guards. I agreed to the injections. Even though I was insane I could still sense immediate fear and danger. My mind still alerted me to the fact that the security guards would force me to be injected if I refused to accept it voluntarily.

Life in the psychiatric ward sometimes had its moments. One night I found myself in the music room where there was an acoustic guitar and an upright piano. I picked up the guitar and started playing a tune which I had penned a few years back. Another patient accompanied me on the piano and we had a great jam session. The rest of the patients were cheering along. The place was rocking and rolling. It was beautiful and even the staff joined in the frivolity. For a brief moment in time music protected our minds from wandering and we synchronised freedom of expression. That all came to an abrupt halt when one of the nurses tried to play 'Flight of the Bumblebee' by Nikolai

Rimsky-Korsakov on the piano. He killed the mood and I winced with every clumsily missed note. Total tosser!

This young male nurse was particularly annoying as I felt he was condescending towards me and this infuriated me to no end. Along with an older male nurse he was driving me crazy. Whilst playing chess with the young male I had a fleeting thought of stabbing him in the head with the pointy end of the bishop I had just acquired. I didn't, though.

The older male nurse had a more direct tone and I found him quite rude. He was aware of my illness and should have been equipped with the necessary training and skills to deal with my mood swings and irrational thoughts. Unfortunately, governments neglect mental illness because it is a taboo not openly discussed. As schizophrenia affects approximately one per cent of the world's population (in fact, bipolar afflicts three per cent of the global population), I cannot imagine why this is the case. It is reality, however and mental illness generally falls into the 'neglected' category because it is considered self-inflicted, or a subject not to be discussed at dinner parties. Yet everybody complains about their cholesterol and blood sugar levels being high. It is a silent disabler and should be researched by global governments extensively. If it were not for research I may have had to endure electro-shock treatment for life, instead of popping pills. Let us go back even further in time and my condition may have been treated with a frontal lobotomy. I am sorry, but that's professional medical murder!

It is widely acknowledged by NAMI (National Alliance of Mental Illness), WHO (World Health Organization) and other health organisations that by 2020, depression will become the second largest disease burden globally. Why then is there so little, by comparison to other disabling illnesses, government funding into research?

In any event, the music session was a search for some creative release to eradicate the absolute boredom and monotony of life in the asylum.

I experienced that same musical creative release prior to arriving in the UK. I was alone at our marital home and picked up my electric guitar (Van Halen signature edition). I plugged it into my effects rack and cranked up the Marshall amplifier. As the solid state valves were warming up, I erupted into some fluid playing and my fingers felt like elastic. They were moving of their own accord. I had never played like that before. It was sheer genius. I felt literally possessed by another being which was guiding my fingering and finger-tapping of the guitar. Spiralling arpeggios and monster licks chased each other in my home and I could literally visualise the notes coming off my axe and floating into the night air. It was wickedly fast, crisp and improvised musicality.

That would be one of the last times I would ever play an electric guitar. Upon returning to my parents' home I sold all of my music equipment including an assortment of guitars, effects racks, amplifiers and, yes, one baby grand piano. As I was on a spiritual crusade/journey I knew that these material items would not be of any value to me where I was going. I also had to cleanse myself of all addictions to remain true to objectivity and, unfortunately, in my mind, music was one of them.

This same cleansing sensation was amplified whilst I was living in London. As mentioned earlier, I was a long-time Liverpool supporter and my wife and I made a three-day trip to Merseyside to see the sights and of course, visit Anfield. I took the off-match tour and ended up with the guide in the players' dressing room. The players' numbers were adorning the run of hung pegs. I looked at the one with my least favourite player and looked toward the guide. There was agreement between our minds that this player had to leave. Later that week there would be a newspaper article outlining the imminent departure of that player to another team. My decision was vindicated. I could enforce my authority anywhere and everywhere. I had no boundaries. There were no limits to my superpowers. I was indeed a demigod.

There would be psychological counselling sessions in the institution, which I flatly refused, thinking that there was nothing wrong with me. I would also refuse to participate in the art and craft sessions; papier-mâché? Come on! I would only speak to and confide in my British psychiatrist. I liked him and in my mind determined his profile to be good.

I quickly made friends with some of the Greek patients. We became a band of four. The other three were a lot older than me and had their own issues to deal with. One had tried to commit suicide by swallowing a pair of scissors. We did not get on well because he would not give me cigarettes when I would sometimes run out. The second gentleman was a lot older and was always dressed in pyjamas and believed himself to be Portuguese. He thought that he would embarrass Greek people if they found out he was Greek. The third one was a rather large Greek man who was totally insane, but somehow we bonded in the institution. I was their spiritual psychotic leader.

Once, this large Greek patient emerged from his room with no top on, exposing a rather large hairy chest, and sat next to me in the communal lounge of the High Dependency Unit. He started telling me about his Greek army service stories, including performing fellatio on a fellow soldier. He asked me if the Church would forgive him. I told him that it would be OK, because by now I was virtually controlling the whole Church.

I would enter this man's room whilst he was sleeping to

secretly steal cigarettes from him. I would trade these cigarettes for slices of pizza, which would be routinely ordered by some of the patients on the 'inside'. The cigarette economy!

During one frantic night whilst we were both experiencing hypomanic episodes he asked me for change to use the payphone. I obliged. He called the Greek operator and started rambling on and on about a Balkan war with bordering European countries. He asked them if everything was OK in Greece. The operator who answered the call did not know what was going on but advised him that everything was OK. He must have called over thirty times that night.

Seeing him 'connecting' overseas gave me an idea. So I reverse-charge-called Greece asking relatives about the political situation and telling them that the government of the USA were going to fly me out that night and resettle me in Greece. I must have made a dozen calls before they stopped accepting the charges. It was one wild night!

The large Greek patient and I spent the night reminiscing about our lives and sharing stories. We were sitting outside in the courtyard and we did not get to sleep until much later that morning.

I would catch up with him after both our stints at the institution were served. He would recover a lot slower than me and would still be considerably overweight.

During both my stints in hospital I would mainly refuse to dine with the other patients or eat any of the food provided. I thought that they were coating it with mind-altering drugs and would insist on family and friends supplying regular meals to me on their many visits. On the few occasions where I would eat the food, it would be after everyone else had finished. As mentioned earlier, I would of course indulge in pizza slices when there were some ordered and available. This was one of the few luxuries.

The other patients were a colourful bunch. They would rant and rave about CIA infiltration, Japanese corporations ruling the world and various multi-layered conspiracy theories. There was one rather large jolly man who would be dressed in a three-piece suit waiting for 'the forces' to take him away to paradise. We were all insane and loving every minute of it. The conversations on the inside did not make any sense, nor did they follow any logical progression. They were random attempts to resolve confused thoughts and to try and work out how the hell we had all got here in the first place. The courtyard was our sanctuary as we all tried to find inner peace and harmony there.

One day in the courtyard a young stocky man approached me regarding the book I had been trying to read. It was written in the Greek language and had been handed to me by my mother during one of her many visits. I explained to him that it was about an Orthodox saint and his journey. He asked me if the Greek Orthodox Church would allow him entry even though he was not Orthodox. In my confused state I assumed the mantle of archdiocese and stated that the Church welcomed all believers. The next day he would insult me and tell me forcefully what to do with my Church. That is the paradox of insanity. Your thoughts rotate from day to day and they do not follow any logical arrangement. They are scattered notes on the fretboard of life. Your mood changes rapidly without any reason. Your beliefs alter with whatever your latest ideas and ideals are, or are believed to be.

I avoided the majority of the other patients and decided that my inadvertent clinical admission was one large mistake. I would be free soon and not have to put up with their stupidity, their lack of understanding and their insanity. I was, of course, the chosen one.

I would find it difficult to get to sleep at nights. The controlling forces in my head would make me sleep fully clothed with shoes on. Forty-five minutes or so would pass before they would allow me to take my shoes off. A short time later they would allow me to take my socks and jeans off. The process would continue until I was in my underwear. They also forced me to perform push-ups to keep my body fit. It was just like being in prison. Thought would enter and leave my mind.

I would also rub off the name on the door of my room. It would be scribed with a black marker. Sometimes I would just leave my first name and other times I would become anonymous. The nurses would always rewrite it the next morning. It was infuriating. As was the hourly flashlight into your face to ensure everything was 'OK'.

This was absolute hell. I had to get out. I was not meant for this. Although I wished for my journey to continue, it had to be under my terms! I needed to and yearned to meander into normal life and remain the anonymous, unknown solitary soldier.

One night I was feeling completely sexually aroused and asked for a two-hour evening pass to go watch a movie. The hospital team felt as though at this stage there would be little risk, so they agreed to my request. I caught a cab to the nearest brothel and enjoyed an hour of heightened sexual pleasure with a prostitute. It was vivid, exciting, wild, fetishistic and dangerous. I caught a cab back and on the way back stopped for some take-away food. The cab brought me back to the hospital and that night I slept peacefully. As the taxi driver dropped me off he asked if I was visiting or if I was a patient. I replied that it was a long story. It was one of the most exciting nights of my life. The sheer danger and adrenaline made it a great experience!

I would share similar exhilaration and excitement during my halcyon pre-London, pre-marital days. Enter one Czech Republic bombshell. She was a part-time model with wavy blonde hair and glittering blue eyes. She was picture-perfect. Straight out of a magazine. We dated for three or so months and it was one of the most sexually steamy periods in my life. We would have sex anywhere and at any time. Elevators, movie theatres and the outdoors would be the backdrop to our exploits. I could not get enough and felt possessed by her beauty. The nights would drag into the mornings with non-stop action and excitement. It was like a drug and I had to have more.

I bumped this relationship, or maybe she did, and I moved on to an older Italian woman. She too was experimental and lived on the wild side. We would have sex everywhere, including a football field late one night. I bumped her too because she was getting too close to me personally and, as a guarded individual, I did not like that. She did not take it too well and would call me regularly to get back together. I would not oblige and, knowing that my next affair was just around the corner, I let the relationship die a natural death.

This cycle would continue indefinitely. Looking back, at the time I was just too confident and did not appreciate the emotional complexity of love. I was, and still am, a much-closed person and you could maybe even label me as *cold* in nature. I would prefer to use the terms 'logical' and 'emotionally passive'.

The 'cold' theme plagued me for a while and I recall washing up in a bathroom stall at the airport in Geneva. The cleaning attendant was watching me as I deliberately turned on the cold water, in lieu of the hot water, and cleansed my hands between flights. He smiled warmly and stated, 'Cold water is the best.' I knew he was referring to my personality and endorsing my profile. I smiled back and continued my icy journey.

During my second stay in hospital I began speaking the English language with a very heavy Greek accent. It all started when I was playing billiards in the designated pool room with one of the other patients. He was young and passive and I felt I needed to protect him. His parents would visit him often. For some reason, every time I entered the pool room my accent would become Greek in nature. I am still not sure how this happened. It would eventually become my normal speaking accent and then all of a sudden one day it just disappeared. Even my British psychiatrist asked me to cease using my accent. I could not halt it during the initial onset, though.

When I was employed by the Israeli directors, I encountered other things that, like the pool room, caused an instant shift in my mind. There was one client website which I could not enter because it felt like it crystallised my brain. Every time I tried to land on the home page a sharp pain would strike my left eye. I concluded it was a global corporate barrier put there to stop me accessing secrets I should not be allowed to view. I tried other Internet paths to access the website. Nope, same effect!

The television in the asylum was old and hard to watch as the picture was slightly blurred. I therefore spent a lot of time pacing around the front and back courtyard, trying to clear my mind. The nurses would ask me why I was pacing and I would explain sheepishly that I was just trying to get some exercise. The nurses were also starting to annoy me. They would keep dossiers on activity and mine would invariably read, *The patient seems agitated.* Yeah, no joke!

I would play Scrabble and chess with some of the nurses just to pass the time. I would cheat at Scrabble by sneaking a look into the available letter bag when the nurse wasn't looking, so I could coincidentally find the letters I required for a high score. She must have known, but I was very discreet. I am sure that went into the dossier also: *The patient habitually cheats at Scrabble.* My dossier was beginning to read like a short story. I was getting more agitated and invented a way to cheat at chess also. Incidentally, I would still lose at both games consistently!

During my sessions with the British psychiatrist, I covered up many of my thought processes as I still believed that they were better served in my own mind than verbally shared with others. I was still paranoid at this stage and convinced that the world would anoint me as some sort of messiah and lavish me with gifts and monetary reward. In fact, one night during my second stay in hospital, I remember telepathically communicating with the general banking fraternity and mentally transferring millions of US dollars into one Swiss bank account and one Swedish bank account. I could feel the transaction being completed in my mind for money I would be due shortly.

The morning after the bank transfer I lay in a dreamy state. I was not quite awake in my bed within the hospital ward when a familiar digitally crisp British voice stated in a matter-of-fact tone, 'Your transaction is complete.' I rose from my bed immediately, not knowing if I was dreaming or awake. The warm voice was familiar to me. It was the same voice that had pinned Cambridge University back at the London train station. Despite the apparent volume of the spoken words I knew I was the only one who could hear the phrase. I smiled to myself knowing that I would soon be free to continue my psychotic journey, all the while accompanied by a heavenly English angel. My guardian angel.

Sixteen

I was eventually released from the hospital on a strict community compliance order. I would have to report to a government psychiatrist and be injected every two weeks with a heavy dosage of medication. This would inevitably zone me out, as would the realisation that the world I had created in my mind did not actually exist.

The weeks turned into months and years. I was sleeping a lot, had no motivation and was aimless in any pursuit of life or meaning. The multiple government psychiatrists I reported to were just that, bureaucrats! Boring government employees who had no real grasp on rehabilitation. There was one Indian psychiatrist who at the end of every session would repeat the same stupid passing comment: 'Lose some weight and get a job.' He was particularly annoying as he would always be running late and his command of the English language was limited. It was his second language and he tended to mumble. I literally dreaded each session with him.

I remember this life hiatus as immensely depressing and very challenging. I avoided socialising with friends because, dare I say it, I was embarrassed by my disease. I felt weak and tarnished. What you need to understand is that what I spent my whole life believing to be reality and the norm was in fact a fabricated existence concocted in my mind during my altered state. The painfully boring realisation that I was ill and the process of coming to grips with this new reality were a real drag. I kept on thinking about what had happened and trying to resolve it logically in my, now somewhat sane, mind. Try as I might I could not. It was all too large a task and I found salvation in television and junk food.

I would go out with friends and family now and then, but it was not the same. I was dark and gloomy, and my head space was miles away. Even cognitive learning and reasoning were painstakingly difficult. I would start books and not finish them. Movies would be hard to follow and my zest for life was slowly dissipating. I could not think clearly and I just did not wish to engage. I was void of any identity or personality profile. I was basically just existing.

You need to realise that what I believed to be my identity was merely a collection of disjointed thoughts manipulated by abnormally low levels of glutamate receptors. So who was I and what was my path going to be? I had to piece together the fragmented history of myself and let my genetics and environmental factors determine who I was and who I was going to be.

The multiple government employment agencies I was referred to were similar to the multiple government psychiatrists treating me: bureaucratic and with no idea about the real world or about real assistance. Fed up with one of these employment agencies, I asked to be released from their register to a different agency, which was introduced to me by a relative. Why did I wish to leave the previous agency? Their theory was that if I wished to work full-time then I should search for work full-time. They wanted me to spend forty to fifty hours a week looking for work. Don't get me wrong; they were not rude, just incredibly out of touch.

I would eventually find a job of my own accord and when I advised the agencies of my successful application they began fighting each other to claim the job position as their own acquisition. It was hilarious, as they had not directly assisted in any way. They must have had to meet government placement targets to pay for all of their morning caffè lattes, cappuccinos and muffins, as their bums got bigger sitting on those expensive taxpayer-funded chairs.

It was only by opening up to family and friends that I overcame the debilitating illness. I started slowly, recalling psychotic events with those close to me. I would outline my thoughts during those moments. To my surprise my confiding circle did not reject me as an outcast but embraced my storytelling, as we shared laughter over the retelling of humorous incidents. The more I opened up, the more comfortable I felt about my disease. It was a liberating experience and my confidence would grow with every interaction.

If pressed now I could document and trace my progress to normality via an event timeline. I also am acutely aware now that I cannot stand alone. As a social creature I need a support network made up of family, friends and medical practitioners to guide me through life. Whilst in cyberspace, though, I believed that I would continue a fantastic solo journey until the end of time.

The government mental health department would release me, albeit begrudgingly, from my community compliance order and allow me to revert to prescription-based medication. This was one of the few victories for me after many years. I recall making countless release applications to a board made up of lawyers and psychiatrists, only to be rejected countless times.

When I was eventually released back into society, so to speak, I remember having schizophrenic nightmares. I would wake up in a pool of sweat with abnormal recollections of the night's visions. The recollections would include me becoming psychotic because the medication was not taking effect. I would be floating over my bed with the same historic psychotic frame of mind. I would always wake up at the exact time my current and former, psychotic, self would meet. Mind the gap!

I asked to be reinstated on the government programme with a psychiatrist, but as I had been released to a GP, they refused assistance. These same muppets that had taken freedom from me, against my will, now refused to assist me.

My GP referred me to my current psychiatrist. This private psychiatrist spent months trying to recover my file from the government psychiatrists, who initially refused to relinquish it. They eventually released it to him and to my dismay it had entries which not only were inaccurate, but referred to me as an alcoholic and a drug abuser. I only drink socially and they would not have known anything about any of my recreational drug habits. They had obviously cut and pasted from somebody else's file, or simply got it altogether wrong. It is quite astonishing to consider that your psychiatric medical history could be incorrectly transcribed. Furthermore, I had asked repeatedly for it to be adjusted to reflect the truth. The government psychiatrists had concurred and assured me that the errors would be corrected. They never were. Do not have blind faith in the system that surrounds and governs you, as it may be prone to errors. It is definitely not absolute!

In fact, 'nothing is absolute', as stated to me by a lady I met whilst playing blackjack at the Loutraki Casino in Greece. I was winning a considerable amount of money and for some reason, upon vacating her seat to avoid a heavy loss, she directed the comment to me in a matter-of-fact tone. She was considerably older than me, but nevertheless very attractive. Why would she say that? It stuck with me for quite some time, hovering in my mind like a curse, until I violently unleashed it on that Credit Suisse recruitment consultant. I directly informed her that Swiss behaviour was not absolute and slammed the hotel phone down hard, destroying the receiver. I did not pay for the repairs. For you see, in my mind, I was trying to eliminate all tagging of thought and commentary that would slow me down in my ascending journey. The burden of nothing being absolute was one more item I had to release in an unexpected, unsolicited manner. I did not want anyone or anything hovering over me and dragging me down.

Nightmares like the ones I suffered after my release also plagued my childhood. From early memory, I recall dreaming of an old lady with tattooed forearms asking if she could make my parents' home a place of God. This dream would recur multiple times, and although I did not know it at the time, it was a schizophrenic dream. The colours were vivid and the voice was digitally clear. It was like a high-definition horror movie! OK, so maybe I was born schizophrenic and it eventually overran my mind. This gradual progression over a number of years would explain much about my early development. We will never know, though!

Same childhood, different recurring nightmare. I would enter my bedroom and standing before me would be a very large, muscular red-blazoned devil with his back to me. The image was similar to, and yet much more frightening than, the mythological creature depicted by artists throughout history. Horns affixed to each of his temples, he would turn around and instruct me to 'Get out!' in demonic tones. The devil's colours were vivid and a shade of red I could not even begin to describe. With eyes of fire he would haunt me for a long time. I would always awake from my sleep as he cut loose with his tirade and would assure myself it was nothing but a dream!

I would return to a fairly normal life, thanks in no small part to my current privately appointed psychiatrist. From the first time I called him, he insisted that he would only take me on if I was compliant with medication. I knew from his tone right then that he was the real deal. I agreed on the matter of compliance and from that point on I knew that I would be on some sort of medication for life, with all its associated side effects.

I would much later research the subject of schizophrenia in lengthy detail just to see what science had to say about my condition. My private psychiatrist and I would passionately debate whether I was bipolar afflicted or paranoid schizophrenic. I leant toward the latter. My long-time private psychiatrist resolved my condition as bipolar and on the cusp of schizophrenia. It did not matter as I possessed all of the symptoms.

Dating women, post the psychological apocalypse, was an interesting experience and sometimes very humorous. My inner circle would set me up with blind dates regularly. The respective lady and I would speak on the phone and then agree to meet on a date at a location close to both our residences. I recall two first date nights.

Blind date one: I called the designated lady after she had agreed to pass on her telephone details to my auntie (Mum's sister), who knew her mother from a third party. We chatted briefly over the phone. As we were practically family friends, we agreed to convene at her apartment. She felt comfortable with me coming over. I arrived and we exchanged cheek kisses. The routine pleasantries followed and then we started conversing about our past and life in general.

I told her that my career trajectory had been interrupted by a private illness and I considered it a minor stumbling point in my life. I thought she would let the subject go, as I had glossed over it, referring to it as a small bump on the highway. She didn't let it go, though. She was probing me further and further for an explanation of my private illness.

I stated candidly that it was bipolar. There was momentary silence. The mood darkened as we took sips of our coffee, prepared earlier by the inquisitive female. I outlined some of the events of my multiple psychotic episodes. Dare I say it, she did not embrace my humorous recollection of the schizophrenic diaries. I am sure she was thinking, *There is no way I will be dating this nutcase.* It went silent for what seemed like an eternity.

An hour and a half or so had passed when I decided to leave and it was fairly mutually transmitted, by the mood, that we would not embark on a relationship. In hindsight it was the first time I had felt mental illness prejudice. I had summoned the nerve and courage to contact her and now felt deflated that there could possibly be prejudice toward my disease. I decided then and there that I would not reveal my affliction to anyone outside my circle, unless the relationship, platonic or otherwise, was going to develop and mature.

Blind date two: my parents were commissioning some electrical service work in their house and the attending employees included the company's receptionist. I was at work at the time. My mother engaged the receptionist in conversation, which led to the introduction of myself, and they agreed on a future date between us. The receptionist left her contact details behind.

We convened at a café in between both our residences, but closer to hers. My mother had described her as 'breathtaking and really nice'. She was neither breathtaking nor nice. Now, I do not regularly objectify women, but she was carrying way too many pounds and was not the beautiful princess my mother had built her up to be.

We chatted for a while and I was getting really bored. We had ordered coffees and I asked her if she would like a dessert. She stated she could not possibly have one, as she was watching her figure. I asked her again encouragingly and she reluctantly agreed. 'Waiter. Two strawberry mille feuille, please.'

The desserts arrived and she took a small bite from the rather large cake as I slowly ate away at my portion. She was about a quarter of the way through it and stated that she could not possibly eat any more. I found this hard to believe, unless she had started her diet that night; she had been down the cake path regularly. Still the mille feuille lay there waiting for some attention.

The night wrapped up within the hour, as I knew from our first exchange that we would not be embarking on an endless love. As we agreed to wind up the evening, I asked her to finish off the cake. Again, she stated that she was full. I said, 'Go on. Come on.' To my surprise, as I cranked my now stiff neck to the left, she devoured it in one fell swoop, leaving nothing on the plate. The poor mille feuille never stood a chance. I recounted the evening's events to a close friend of mine and we laughed and laughed the whole night.

So one may deduce that I was being punished for my skirt-chasing youthful years. I was young, arrogant and extremely confident around women. With an insatiable appetite I craved chance female encounters and exhaustive interpersonal sessions.

Scene one from my late teenage years: a friend of mine had his parents' house available for a weekend as his parents were away on some retreat. We did not give it a second thought. We were going to carve up the house and get into as much mischief as possible.

Early on in the week my friend and I had picked up some girls from a local eatery, in preparation for a wild night that weekend. As we had little to time to meet new women we agreed to take these two on the weekend bender. We had exchanged phone numbers and agreed to meet them in town. The ladies would then drive the whole party of four to my friend's parents' house. Unknown to our female companions, we had pre-planned for three other friends to hide in the house whilst we got busy with the ladies.

The girls were a little overweight and not quite supermodels. Perfect! In any event we paired off. Our three other friends began to make ghost noises from their hiding places in the house, getting progressively louder. This freaked the women out a little and we reassured them that it was just the wind outside.

My friend and I had paired off in different rooms in the house. We had pre-agreed with our other three friends that they would scare our partners when we were all undressed by jumping out from their hiding closets. They did just that and it was funny to us but not so funny for the girls.

What my friend and I did not know was that one of our other three friends had let down one of their tyres. The same friend who had handed me the Oxford T-shirt.

The girls were going to give us a ride into town. After they dressed quickly in embarrassment, we all hopped into their car. We drove for about half a kilometre before the car stalled, due to the flat tyre. We did not know what to do, but we all exited the vehicle. To our surprise the boot of the car had a broken lock so we could not open it to retrieve the spare.

A truck pulled over and a gentleman with a hook for one hand hopped out and walked towards us. It was a slow deliberate walk and he had a slight limp. In the dark night he cut quite a scary image. We were all petrified. With his hooked arm he prised open the boot compartment and assisted us by changing the tyre.

The above is all true and happened exactly as stated. The hook-handed man was a really nice truck driver. At the time, though, we thought he was coming out of his vehicle to harm us. The five of us lads are all still friends now and laugh at this story constantly every time we mention it.

Scene two from my late teenage years: I had been dating an older Italian woman for a short while and it was quite a vivacious love affair. It was steaming up and getting quite wild. We agreed to convene at a friend of mine's house for the night. Similar to my other friend, his parents were also gone for a weekend. He also invited another one of our male friends.

My older Italian girlfriend wanted to bring one of her girlfriends along for the following session of debauchery. Her girlfriend was completely out there and, if I may state, quite weird. She was always wearing dark makeup and was not as outgoing as my Italian girlfriend. I arranged to pick them up from their respective homes and drive them to my friend's parents' home. My other friend was already there when we arrived. We were three men and two women.

We started by having a few drinks to loosen up. I polished off three quarters of a bottle of whisky and very soon was completely inebriated. I was getting it on with my girlfriend on the couch of the lounge room whilst my two friends were trading alpha male stories with the other female in the kitchen, jostling for rites of passage.

For some reason I ended up naked and decide to run around the house totally confused and totally nude. My girlfriend interrupted my merry little dance and led me to my friend's bedroom, where we continued our makeout session. We were both very excited and consummated the evening very erotically.

After the act I started feeling ill and the room began spinning violently. I turned to my left and hurled up the week's food. My girlfriend was not amused and asked my host friend to drive her and her friend back home. He did so, of course. When he returned I was feeling slightly better and we decided to take the mattress out so it could freshen up. What we did not count on was the sleeping dog getting a smell of the soaked mattress.

I am not sure where I eventually slept that night, but somehow I made it to work the next day, late of course. I received a call from my friend stating that his dog had torn the mattress to shreds and his parents were coming home soon. What was he going to tell them? His parents were furious and asked him to explain why he had taken the mattress out for an airing. His feeble defence fell apart. Many years later it is still one of our favourite stories.

During this time, schizophrenia or not, I was a real arrogant prick! Did the heavens punish me for past misdeeds? It makes you wonder. It makes me wonder. Was my bipolar a balancing for my past acts? Did God have it in for me? Did I deserve it? I do not believe youthful pranks anger God to the point of retribution. Science defines my condition as being attributed to a chemical imbalance. Whatever! I did once, however, have a brain scan which did not reveal anything conclusively. Damn! Unscientifically cursed for life.

Prescription medication, from memory, went through the following procession: Risperdal (risperidone), olanzapine and currently Abilify (aripiprazole) with an 'over the counter' brain stimulant. There would always be a new drug on the market which would supersede the previous one. My next step would have been the drug used by celebrities known as lithium. However, with a high percentage chance of developing a thyroid disorder, my doctor and I ruled this one out. We would stick to our current cocktail.

And, of course, I would inevitably develop type two diabetes from the weight gain and lack of exercise. You've got to love life's curveballs!

I am as sharp as ever and probably a better person now. I am no longer arrogant and am more appreciative of life and people. I am losing much of the weight I gained and am re-employed with my historic employer of choice. The diabetes is somewhat manageable and I am coping with my gambling addiction.

I live in a stylish apartment in a very nice location and even managed a return trip to Europe, on my own. I travelled to London, Brussels, Bruges, Genk and Athens. Whilst the magic was not the same, I still visited my old Islington flat and retraced my manic footsteps. No, I did not use the left-hand side of Liverpool Street station.

These days the dreams are not as vivid and the voices in my head ceased a long time ago. The closest I get to digital clarity is the voice of one of my clients, at the end of the very expensive handset sitting on my office desk. My stylish one-bedroom apartment is my home and I plough through life like every other slob, 'alone and regrettably sane'. Bills to pay, chores to be completed and a painfully normal version of events. The hypomania and depression have been replaced by mood-stabilising drugs, which do just that: make the everyday boring and mundane, but somewhat manageable. This is life?

The rollercoaster is over and the realisation of growing old and eventually decaying in some nursing home, whilst not obsessing my thoughts, is nevertheless reality. Our time on Earth is but a flickering light waiting to be extinguished by the inevitability of the cycle of life. Once you come to terms with your mortality and your sanity then you can reason out your existence thus far. Fate or divine intervention? Lucky or unlucky? I only wish I knew the answers. Answers to questions which plague all of mankind. Who am I? Where am I going? What is my purpose in life?

Did I indulge in marijuana? Regularly. Did I take mushrooms? Once, administered in a very large taco – that was the mother of all parties in Denver, Colorado, USA. Did I snort cocaine? Of course – same party! Did I take amphetamines? Once or twice. Hash? No other way to enjoy Amsterdam.

The question still beckons. Would I trade my highs and lows for a normal stable life? I don't know. I just don't know. It is what it is and is best summed up by my variation on Descartes' famous phrase, which I sent to the Sorbonne from my London flat via Royal Mail – with no stamp – at the height of my manic-depression:

> *... I thought therefore I was.*
> *I am therefore I am.*
> *I think therefore I will be ...*

Embrace humanity!

> *O Fortune,*
> *like the moon*
> *you are changeable,*
> *ever waxing*
> *and waning;*
> *hateful life*
> *first oppresses*
> *and then soothes*
> *as fancy takes it;*
> *poverty*
> *and power*
> *it melts them like ice.*
>
> *Fate – monstrous*
> *and empty,*
> *you whirling wheel,*
> *you are malevolent,*
> *well-being is vain*
> *and always fades to nothing,*
> *shadowed*
> *and veiled*

you plague me too;
now through the game
I bring my bare back
to your villainy.

Fate is against me
in health
and virtue
driven on
and weighted down,
always enslaved.
So at this hour
without delay
pluck the vibrating strings;
since Fate
strikes down the strong man,
everyone weep with me!

'O Fortuna', circa 13th century AD

Acknowledgements

Many thanks to the support of my inner circle who provided solace during those bleak times.

My private psychiatrist who assisted me with post-episode therapy and ignited the flame which became the book's endless eminence.

Technology companies whose products never failed me over multiple versions of the manuscript.